CW01645627

In *Clothed with Strength*, Sarah
of God working powerfully
women in different places and times in history. She weaves a narrative that is wonderfully readable yet full of a historian's nuance and detail, helping us as modern readers to grasp the challenging times in which they lived as well as their unique gifts and frail humanity through which God chose to work. Read this book — and share it with others — to be encouraged to speak of Christ and show his mercy, whoever you are and wherever you find yourself.

Jen Charteris, Executive Director, Crosslands

Clothed with Strength is a fantastic and fascinating book, recounting the lives of four contrasting women whose stories interweave, all connected by the common thread of Christ's transforming power. Sarah Allen relates their achievements and struggles with compassion and understanding, as well as an awareness of the wider historical movements that formed the background of their lives. Yet it is all done with a lightness of touch. I was moved to tears more than once. These four stories cover the period in which our modern world was formed and speak powerfully to issues of race and class. Above all, they will inspire you to follow Christ.

Tim Chester, author of several Bitesize Biographies including *Mary Jones*

Throughout Christian history, faithful and strong women have served the Lord. All too often, sadly, their stories have faded into obscurity. Here, Sarah Allen introduces us to four of those women whose lives spanned two centuries and half the world. Freed woman and gifted evangelist, Rebecca Protten, is followed by writer and activist, Hannah More. We learn about Ellen Ranyard's army of Bible Women and Josephine Butler's work for and on behalf of many women, including those who were sexually abused, assaulted and forced into prostitution. In the pages of this book, again and again we see their courage and their faith. They did not hesitate to put their faith into practice, no matter what it cost them. The challenge for us is simple: will we do the same?

Ros Clarke, Associate Director, Church Society

Jesus Christ calls us to repent, believe, and to live out our faith. 'Faith without works is dead' (James 2:17). Sarah Allen has provided a compelling account of four women who, in very different contexts, lived out their love for God as they served others. Their stories challenge us, in our day, to fulfil our calling to be salt and light in a corrupt and dark society. But they also inspire us to see that God is well able to supply the resources we need to fulfil that call.

Sharon James, author and Social Policy Analyst, The Christian Institute

CLOTHED WITH STRENGTH

Women who built the church and changed the world

SARAH ALLEN

10 Publishing
a division of 10ofthose.com

Unless otherwise stated, Scripture quotations are from the Holy Bible, New International Version® Anglicized, NIV®. Copyright © 1979, 1984, 2011 by Biblica, Inc.® Used by permission. All rights reserved.

Copyright © 2023 by Sarah Allen

First published in Great Britain in 2023

The right of Sarah Allen to be identified as the Author of this Work has been asserted by her in accordance with the Copyright, Designs and Patents Act 1988.

All rights reserved. No part of this publication may be reproduced, stored in a retrieval system or transmitted in any form or by any means, electronic, mechanical, photocopying, recording or otherwise, without the prior permission of the publisher or the Copyright Licensing Agency.

British Library Cataloguing in Publication Data
A record for this book is available from the British Library

ISBN: 9781913896539

Designed by Jude May
Cover image © Margaret Diemidova | iStock

Printed in Denmark

10Publishing, a division of 10ofthose.com
Unit C, Tomlinson Road, Leyland, PR25 2DY, England
Email: info@10ofthose.com
Website: www.10ofthose.com

1 3 5 7 10 8 6 4 2

FOR JEMIMAH

Contents

Timeline

	1670s	Enslaved Africans arrive on Antigua & St Thomas
	c. 1718	Shelly (later Rebecca Protten) is born on Antigua
	Early 1720s	Rebecca (RP) taken to St Thomas
	Early 1730s	RP baptised and set free
	1738	RP marries Matthaus Freundlich; arrested and imprisoned
	1739	RP released
	1739	Great Awakening begins in New England
	1741	RP travels to Germany; Matthaus dies
Hannah More (HM) born near Bristol	1745	
	1746	RP marries Christian Protten
HM & sisters establish a school	1758	
HM writes *The Search for Happiness*	1763	
	1764	RP moves to the Gold Coast
HM engaged to William Turner	1767	
HM breaks off engagement	1773	
	1775-1776	American War of Independence
	1780	RP dies in the Gold Coast
HM meets John Newton & becomes Christian	1780-1781	
HM establishes network of schools	1789	

	1789-1799	French Revolution
	1807	Abolition of the British slave trade
	1810	Ellen White (later Ranyard) born in London
	1826	Ellen (ER) is converted
Josephine Grey (later Butler) born in Northumberland	1828	
HM dies in Bristol	1833	Abolition of slavery in British territories
	1837	Queen Victoria ascends to throne
	1839	ER marries Benjamin Ranyard
Josephine (JB) marries George Butler; moves to Oxford	1852	ER publishes *The Book and Its Story*
	1857	ER founds the London Bible and Domestic Female Mission
American Civil War	1861-1865	
Eva Butler dies aged 5	1864	
	1865	Salvation Army founded
	1868	ER's mission extends to include nursing
JB founds the Ladies National Association	1870	Oxford University exams opened to women
	1879	ER dies
JB & others expose child prostitution in England	1885	
	1886	Contagious Diseases Act repealed
George Butler dies	1890	
	1901	Edward VII ascends to the throne
JB dies	1906	
	1918	All men & some women gain the vote

Introduction

Twelve generations ago, at the beginning of the eighteenth century, a woman from the African Gold Coast was taken in chains across the Atlantic. Two hundred years later, another woman lay dying in London, worn out by hard-fought battles for social transformation.

Between these two points in history the world changed beyond recognition. Colonial empires expanded, slavery was outlawed and the United States gained independence. From steam engines to trains and street lights, everyday life was transformed by technology. The world became smaller, communication became easier and the industrial era was born.

This book details the lives of four women during this period: Rebecca Protten, Hannah More, Ellen Ranyard and Josephine Butler. While the two centuries in which they lived saw dramatic cultural and spiritual change, what draws these women together is their God-given drive to fight injustice, help the oppressed and seek the transformation of society through the offer of salvation in Jesus.

Like the noble wife described in Proverbs, all four women had 'faithful instruction' on their tongues and opened their 'arms to the poor'. In doing so they established patterns for women's ministry which we still see today. Rebecca Protten, a freed slave, was set aside as a worker by the church, standing strong despite being jailed. Hannah More used her fame as a popular author to transform British attitudes to slavery and promote education amongst the emerging working classes. Ellen Ranyard pioneered the training of underprivileged women as evangelists in the slums of London. Josephine Butler campaigned against state-sanctioned prostitution and child abuse, bringing to light the evils of nineteenth-century culture. These four women may not be well known today, but their influence can still be felt.

In a world where we are encouraged to claim our power and shout about our identity, these women teach us what it means to lay aside the significant privilege of wealth, reputation and freedom. They show us how a powerful God delights to use his people's weakness. Their identity was in him and they did not fight for their own rights but for his glory and the good of others. In that sense, this book is his story, not theirs. We should honour them for their work but remember that they lived and served clothed in his strength.

My prayer is that this book would inspire us to do the same.

She is clothed with strength and dignity;
she can laugh at the days to come.
She speaks with wisdom,
and faithful instruction is on her tongue …

Charm is deceptive, and beauty is fleeting;
but a woman who fears the LORD *is to be praised.*
Honour her for all that her hands have done,
and let her works bring her praise at the city gate.

(Proverbs 31:25–31)

Servant of the Enslaved

REBECCA PROTTEN,

1718-1780

1

Beginnings

Only one picture of Rebecca Protten exists. In her mid-thirties, Rebecca sits upright beside her husband, plainly clothed in a dark dress, white scarf and close-fitting white cap, with blue ribbons to mark her married status. Her dark skin contrasts with that of her little two-year-old daughter, Anna Maria, who sits between them, naked to the waist, one hand raised in greeting. What Rebecca thought about being painted is hard to tell. Her lips are almost smiling, her gaze is intelligent and confident, but she gives little away.

Very few records of her life remain, and the only place we can hear her own voice is in fragments of three letters which have survived. She owned next to nothing and founded no movements. Rebecca may be to some degree a mystery, but her life is important because of how God used her, and others like her in the eighteenth century. Born a slave in Antigua, Rebecca was at the heart of an extraordinary movement of God, the fruits of which are still being formed today.

The eighteenth century was a time of significant change. The industrial revolution was beginning to disrupt ancient ways of life, as manufacturing moved out of cottage workshops and into factories. Much of this development was financed by the Atlantic trade in human lives: cheap mass-produced goods were taken to Africa to exchange for slaves, and the wealth that poured back into Britain could be invested in new businesses. Away from industry, philosophers were challenging traditional concepts of truth and knowledge while at the same time some churches were rediscovering the message of justification by faith and finding new ways of sharing this through outdoor preaching and small Bible classes.

Rebecca's story, shadowy though it is, shows us something of how, in the midst of all these other changes, the Protestant church was developing its ideas on how women could serve.

Of course, throughout history, women have served God. Before the Reformation in the first half of the sixteenth century, many nuns were scholars and writers whose works were treasured by the church. Then there were the faithful noblewomen, princesses and queens who were involved in politics. They used their influence to support the church and its teachings. And beyond these, there are the many, many unknown girls, women, wives and mothers who spoke of Christ to others, cared for the sick, visited those in prison and counselled the suffering. Rebecca Protten has much in common with the women who came before her, but she is also an example of a different kind of service, showing us how what we now call evangelicalism changed the way women worked.

Rebecca's story starts and finishes in the Gold Coast of Africa, now known as Ghana. In the early eighteenth century, the coastline was punctuated by forts built by traders who controlled the seas. Between the white sand and the scrubland of the shoreline you can still see white painted walls with high battlements. Behind these walls are spacious living apartments and dark holding cells. Today they are empty, with only information boards to tell visitors their violent stories. The forts' names and architecture reveal the successive waves of Europeans who came to dominate the coast: first the Portuguese in the sixteenth century, then the Dutch and the Danish before finally the British in the nineteenth century.

In the eighteenth century, inland from the forts was a huge area of dry plateaus and tropical forests controlled by the Asante Empire. This powerful and highly organised group had gained its power through selling gold to European merchants, but later had begun to supply slaves in return for firearms. Rebecca Protten's mother was one of these slaves. We don't know anything about her, but we do know a little about the culture she was from and what her journey west must have been like. Nearly all people who were exported like livestock from West Africa had been seized from a village, where huts clustered together, each housing an extended family. The head of the household was the man, and he might have several wives. The women cooked and made pots, they wove, cared for their children and tended crops close to the village. There were hardships – fighting with neighbouring villages, illness and bad weather could destroy lives – but village life had its settled routines.

Christianity has been present in Africa since the earliest days of the church. Great theologians and martyrs from North Africa have blessed generations of believers before Islam arrived from Arabia. Much later, as trade routes opened up, Catholicism brought teaching about Christ into West Africa. Despite this, by the eighteenth century, Christians were a very small minority in the continent; the vast majority of villages followed traditional religion, with its many gods and spirits. They believed trees, plants and even inanimate objects had their own spiritual force. Ancestors exerted great power. The gods could be pleased or angered, and needed keeping happy through rituals as well as charms made of shells or leaves, metal or pottery. A male witch could get you access to their blessings; female prophets could bring you their message.

It was from this world that Rebecca's mother was torn. She was marched to a looming stone fort, to the sea she had probably never seen before, and onto a ship where she was kept in the terrifying darkness of the hold. Four hundred or so people from different areas with different languages were thrust together in one ship for up to eight weeks. The men outnumbering women two to one. The women weren't shackled, like the men, but they too only had one meagre meal a day. Though the traders tried to preserve their valuable cargo, allowing the slaves some time on deck and attempting to ventilate the stinking holds, many died of disease and some even succeeded in suicide. There was no wonder that despair so often set in; Rebecca's mother must have had no idea where she was going. She wouldn't have known how long she must be kept prisoner or whether she would ever see her family again. Had she known the truth, any remaining hope would have died.

Born into bondage

When Rebecca's mother emerged from the stinking slave ship she must have been bewildered. Never having seen the sea before this journey, now she was back on land. The white beaches of Antigua may have looked similar to those back in Ghana, but this certainly wasn't home. She went from the captivity of the hold to a marketplace. The price for a female slave in the early 1700s was likely to have been about $2600 in today's money. Back in Britain, a person could buy four horses for the same money. It was less than for a male slave, because women couldn't do some of the more demanding physical labour and weren't going to be trained in a craft, like carpentry or blacksmithing, unlike some of the men.

Rebecca's mother, if she was young and fit, may have been put in the 'first gang' doing the hardest physical work. From a distance, the vibrant green of sugar cane looks lush and healthy, especially against the blue skies and distant mountains of a Caribbean island. But growing sugar cane in the eighteenth century was a cruel process. The sugar cane was closely planted in trenches by hand and needed to be manured, again by hand, so that it would grow high, over ten feet tall, towering over the harvesters who would come with machetes to cut the thick stems at the ground. Then the cane needed to be hauled away to mills which operated twenty-four hours a day. There, cane was crushed and the juices boiled in coppers. The furious heat and machinery made this the most dangerous part of all. With several harvests a year, there was no rest. No wonder people who'd been enslaved died within a few years of arriving.

There were other tasks Rebecca's mother could have done. Perhaps she worked in a plantation house or in the second gang, weeding the cane fields and picking stones. Whatever her role, the work was relentless, lasting from dawn until dusk, and in the midst of this exhausting round, Rebecca's mother became pregnant. Rebecca's father was white, which means that Rebecca's mother could have had no choice in her sexual relationship with him. In 1718, Rebecca began life in a one room hut. With no medical care, little time for her mother to recover and born into imprisonment, this was a hard beginning. Her childhood would be very short.

The baby was named Shelly, and it was only later she became Rebecca. For six or seven years, little Rebecca managed to stay with her mother. There was only straw to sleep on and food wasn't plentiful. Perhaps there were other children around to play with while her mother worked, perhaps she had siblings, though the harsh conditions of the enslaved women's lives meant that most children died in their first seven years. Rebecca was one of the hardy ones and so she was marked out for work even when she was small. In an achingly sad repetition of history, Rebecca was stolen away, put on a ship and taken to a different island to be sold. She may have been sold by the plantation owners or taken by some kind of pirates. When Rebecca told the story of her early years to others, she described being kidnapped; the trauma of separation was still fresh in her memory. All the later comfort of the gospel and the close friendships with believers from many different places did not erase memories of betrayal and loss.

Rebecca arrived at an island 220 miles away. It was a journey lasting four or five days, shorter than the journey her mother had endured but still full of terror and loss, wrenched from her mother and her home, travelling to an unknown future. St Thomas, now part of the US Virgin Islands, was at least not too different from Antigua. It was a small Danish colony, with sugar plantations around the perimeter and a mountainous inner terrain. Familiarity with the landscape couldn't have fully prepared Rebecca for the squalor of a slave market and the transition from plantation life to becoming a domestic slave of a prominent family. She was on her own, away from her mother, the safety of their hut and the company she knew. She was only six or seven years old.

A new name

Her new master, Lucas Van Beverhout, was probably the third or fourth generation of an elite family on the island. Creoles, the long-term white settlers, had a reputation for harshness and laziness but he and his family treated Rebecca well. How strange it must have been to be shunted from the dust and dirt around her mother's cabin to a stone-built house. From a place where she spoke her mother tongue and heard overseers shout in English, to a world where cultivated Dutch was spoken. Rebecca was now serving an outpost where, despite the blistering heat and the brutal labour outside, Creoles clung to European manners and customs. In the house women embroidered and read books. There was music and parties, and a religion very different from the rituals and charms or Folk Catholicism remembered by the Africans. Rebecca had so much to learn. The house with its mahogany panelling and fine furniture, mirrors and curtains had to be kept clean, and strange, imported foods had to be cooked. She would have had to learn how to speak this new language to her owners, how to appear invisible and who to trust, as well as who should be avoided.

Rebecca may have been taken on by the Van Beverhouts because she had dual white European and black African heritage. This growing group were cultivated as a kind of buffer between the slaves and their masters. To those who believed Africans were an inferior race, biracial people seemed more biddable and easily moulded, their European features more presentable inside the house. Being given privileges the plantation slaves didn't get meant that they would prove loyal, an important source of security when whites were so vastly outnumbered and news of slave revolts on neighbouring islands stirred real anxiety.

Rebecca was relatively well treated, and even seemed at home with them as the years went on. Someone in the Van Beverhout household taught Rebecca to read and write during those first few years. It wasn't necessary for whatever domestic work she was employed to do; cleaning, laundry and cooking required practical skill but not literacy. She must have been quick about her tasks and quick to pick up the new language to have been noticed among the group of slaves and given teaching. The family must have had some care for their workers to allow this young girl to take time away from her tasks to learn while it was still light or to use a precious candle to study by after dark.

Many children at the time learnt to read by looking at a Bible, painstakingly picking out the letters and piecing them into words. In fact, the Bible could well have been the very reason Rebecca was taught to read. Most employers were very reluctant to let their forced-labourers hear about Christianity, as we'll see, because the logic was clear: if anyone turns to Jesus then they become a sister or brother, a sharer in Christ, a partner in the gospel, and how then can they be enslaved? But the Van Beverhouts were of the Dutch Reformed faith and this church's official stance was that 'the poor and blind pagans' of the Caribbean 'be led to the knowledge of God and their salvation', so in encouraging Rebecca to read and giving her access to the Bible they were following the official line of the church.[1] How

1. Jon Sensbach, 'Slaves to Intolerance', in *The First Prejudice: Religious Tolerance and Intolerance in Early America* ed. Chris Beneke, Christopher S. Grenda (University of Pennsylvania Press, Philadelphia: 2011), 203.

they squared this responsibility with the injustice of owning another human, we can't know.

The Word of God did its work in Rebecca; it became her book. In her teens, she developed a great love for Christ. In one sense, though, little changed. Living as a forgiven person didn't mean living like a European; every night she went back to her hut which she shared with other slaves, her clothes stayed the same, her work was the same, she had to obey commands of her 'superiors' without a murmur. But she did have a new master. She had been bought again, not by gold coins, but by the blood of her Lord. And this purchase was not for work, but for love. Serving the Van Beverhouts would now be secondary. She was under Jesus' loving rule; he was her primary commander; he set her value. And this meant living for him and speaking about him. It was inevitable then that she would want to tell her fellow slaves what she had discovered – that everyone, black or white, was a sinner and needed to be forgiven and be made new.

In the house, Rebecca somehow found a Dutch book of martyr stories and in moments away from work, sat down to read these tales of courage, persecution and pain. Perhaps they resonated with what she witnessed in the slave community, and her own grief at being torn from her mother. Though the martyrs were from a distant time and place, their stories excited and gripped her; these scorned people had found great hope in the face of terrible death and the Lord had brought them comfort. God was using the stories of past work to stir in this young girl a passion to serve those who were already being persecuted, and to prepare her for the pain that her own service would entail. In years to come, her testimony would be added to the story of the church and would be passed on, encouraging others to pray and to leave their homes to serve.

We don't know if Rebecca was allowed to accompany her master's family to church worship, but it seems as though she wasn't able to be baptised there, because when a Catholic priest visited the island she sought him out and Shelly became Rebecca as she was baptised. This step marked her out officially as a Christian and changed her status in the house. Those at the time would protest that it made no economic sense to liberate an enslaved person just at the point of adulthood, physically strong and skilled for all kinds of task, but that is what happened to Rebecca when she was about sixteen. The Van Beverhouts were following the custom, ignored by many, that an African who had been baptised was to be given their freedom.

Much stayed the same for Rebecca. She was particularly valuable in the household, now having the responsibility of being housekeeper even though she was so young. This was a good and safe position to have. Despite her new status, outside of a household's protection she would be vulnerable to sexual assault or financial exploitation. Without savings she could do little on her own. Rebecca carried on working for the family, but now she had a few coins in her purse, a bedroom in the house and a pair of shoes on her feet for the first time. Life had become a little bit more comfortable; she was treated 'not as a servant but as a member of the household'.[2]

Freed people, and these were most often women, were known to be economically ambitious. They worked hard,

2. Christian Oldendorp, *History of the Mission of the Evangelical Brethren on the Caribbean Islands of St. Thomas, St. Croix, and St. John*, translated (Karoma, Ann Arbor: 1987), 315.

set up businesses, bought land and even, though it is hard to believe, sometimes owned enslaved people themselves. Women of dual heritage might aim at having relationships with white men, knowing that it would make their position more secure; for a freed person there always remained a fear of returning to the whip and shackles. Any slip might take them back to captivity. This makes Rebecca's choices all the more extraordinary. For rather than social climbing and securing her own future, she left behind her new privilege and gave herself to the enslaved. In the little pockets of free time she now had, she spoke about Christ, 'admonishing' women 'often to love God and the Saviour'.[3] Before she had ever heard the word, Rebecca had become a missionary.

3. Oldendorp, *History of the Mission of the Evangelical Brethren*, 314.

2

A Difficult Mission

As the seventeenth century turned into the eighteenth, and Rebecca's mother was being led onto a Danish ship to make profit for businessmen, an Austrian Baroness took her tiny grandson, Nikolaus Zinzendorf, to live in her ancestral home. The cold hall of an Austrian castle was very far from the terrifying dark of a ship's hold, and the prospects of a titled white boy radically different from those of an imprisoned black woman, but a thread connects these two individuals. Nikolaus would travel to the Caribbean decades later and there he would meet Rebecca; despite the vast differences in their upbringings, they would be united through shared, ambitious faith.

Nikolaus must have been bewildered and upset by his move to the castle. His father had died and his mother had married again, moving away to another city and leaving this poor two-year-old effectively parentless. But, however intimidating his new environment with its high grey walls and towers, it was a place of culture and welcome. Imagine the setting of a fairy tale: there were liveried servants and wonderful food on the table, rich fabrics decorating draughty halls. Here aristocrats gathered to listen to music and discuss the latest books. His grandmother, Baroness Henrietta Catharina, was an educated and shrewd noblewoman who had become known as a teenager for her Latin and German poetry. As a young woman she communicated with influential thinkers and scientists and through her marriage to Baron Gersdorff she gained power to influence the politics of the region. What was to have more lasting influence than any of these accomplishments, however, was Henrietta's embrace of Christ.

After the Thirty Years' War which brutally ravaged central Europe between 1618 and 1648, causing the death of somewhere between 4.5 and 8 million people, many had turned against state-governed Christianity. The war had tangled up faith and politics, as Protestant states clashed with Catholic powers, and amidst this turbulence, the dominant Lutheran church had become dry and inward-looking. Perhaps as a result, some Protestants wanted to move away from a state-controlled, and therefore political, religion. They thought the Reformation had been left unfinished and wanted to take it further. This group called for a Christianity which engaged the heart, promoted an individual, personal response to Christ and was serious about holiness. They began Bible studies where people could gather to discuss the Word and pray, and much of what they emphasised is still with us today in the form of evangelicalism.

Henrietta embraced this demanding, emotionally engaged Christianity, which we refer to today as pietism. Through the late seventeenth and early eighteenth centuries, when the Salem witch trials were being held in America and the steam engine was being invented in England, she played host to the movement's key theologians, welcoming them to the castle so that she could discuss theology and faith. She learned from them and supported them financially while they gained credibility from her. This connection with wealth and social prestige gave the pietist movement security in the anxious period after the Thirty Years' War. In this stimulating environment, Henrietta grew in her faith and longed to pass it on, supporting Bible translation, writing hymns and setting up a school for girls, so that they could read the Scriptures for themselves. Women may not have had a formal role in the church in the early 1700s, but Henrietta shows us, during these years some godly women had a lasting impact not just on individuals but on the institution itself.

In later life, Nikolaus recalled that he put his trust in Jesus when he was four years old. As a young child, nurtured in an environment of intense spirituality, the thing that excited him the most was 'the doctrine of Jesus Christ and his death and merits'.[1] Henrietta sent him in his teens to an academy led by a pietist, and while there, Nikolaus started what was, in effect, a Christian Union. He called it 'The Order of the Grain of Mustard Seed'. With his friends, he committed to these four radical aims: total commitment to God, pure living, love for others, and reaching Jews and those of other religions with the gospel.

This last aim, which seems such a central concern of church life today, was barely a question for many European Protestants in the sixteenth and seventeenth centuries. The

1. John R. Weinlick, *Count Zinzendorf: The Story of His Life and Leadership in the Renewed Moravian Church*, (Bethlehem, PA and Winston-Salem, NC: Moravian Church in America: 1989) quoted in https://www.moravian.org/wp-content/uploads/sites/2/2020/05/Zinzendorf.pdf

church was so embroiled in theological battles, exhausted by civil wars and political change, that it had largely forgotten the Great Commission – the command to go into all nations to make disciples of Christ. Although Catholic priests continued their journeys into Asia, Africa and the Americas, and puritan settlers had sought to reach the Native Americans, many zealous Protestants echoed the famous lines: 'When God pleases to convert the heathen he will do it without your aid or mine';[2] their eyes were focused on Europe. At the turn of the eighteenth century however, things began to change. In England a mission agency was established and German pietists began a mission to India which fired Nikolaus's imagination. Later, he met Christian David who had travelled to Greenland and North America, seeking to communicate the good news of Christ to indigenous people. Nikolaus's desire to reach the world for Christ, stirred up by stories shared in a chilly Austrian castle, would eventually bring him, a privileged aristocrat, to read about and later meet the daughter of an abused Gold Coast slave.

In 1722, when he was only twenty-one, a tiny group of religious refugees from Bohemia and Moravia arrived in the estate Nikolaus had bought from his grandmother. They were the remnant of a church established by a follower of Jan Hus, a fifteenth-century Czech reformer, whose belief in and preaching of justification by faith predated Martin Luther's. Persecuted in their homelands by Catholic reformers and suffering great

2. Attributed to John Ryland Senior in 1786 as he denounced William Carey's proposals for world mission, although there is some dispute over whether these words were actually uttered (John Appleby, *I Can Plod: William Carey and the Early Years of the First Baptist Missionary Society* (Grace Publications, London: 2007), 62).

hardship because of the war, they were seeking somewhere safe to settle. Nikolaus welcomed them and found that their beliefs fitted with his own pietist convictions. He granted them land on his estate and called it Herrnhut, meaning 'the Lord's shelter'. Others from different Protestant backgrounds joined this new community and after a difficult period of disunity, a communal life of worship and work was established. Nikolaus formally became their leader and patron in 1727 and the movement grew, and with this, Nikolaus's desire to reach the nations for Christ grew too.

It was at the court of the Danish King Christian VI that this vision coalesced. Like many rulers of the time, the king had black servants. One of his portraits shows him, elderly, bewigged and in rather shiny armour, with a young black boy holding his robes. The boy is clearly on display; he has a huge, feathered headdress and pearl earrings, not the usual clothing of a court servant. But servants weren't the only black people present in the court. There in 1731, in the imposing halls of Copenhagen Castle, Nikolaus Zinzendorf met Anthony Ulrich, a man who had been enslaved on St Thomas where Rebecca had her home. Anthony spoke freely in the court about the physical and spiritual oppression of the slaves on the island. Nikolaus took Anthony back with him to his Christian community in Herrnhut to share these stories and appeal for help. There Anthony asked the daring question: Who would go and give their life for this cause? David Nitschmann and Leonhard Dober, both under the age of twenty-five, responded to this call. In keeping with Moravian principles of leadership, they weren't theologians receiving a salary, but in theory, self-supporting craftsmen. They were prepared to work hard and put themselves in danger, travelling far from their home and culture. They were willing, in fact, 'to give their lives as a sacrifice to the will of the Saviour and would gladly become slaves if they could win only one soul for Him', because they assumed that the best way to reach enslaved Africans would be to become like them, working side-by-side on a plantation.[3]

After their journey in the autumn of 1732 – not in the dark hold of a trading ship, but as paying travellers in a cabin – these men found that no one would take them as slaves and that instead, they would have to work within the infrastructure of slavery just to survive on the island. Nitschmann was a skilled carpenter and was able to earn good wages in constructing houses for white plantation owners. Dober found work much harder; his attempts at making pottery and fishing were dismal, but eventually he found well-paying work as a steward to the Colonial Governor. It wasn't an auspicious start and they faced many frustrations; serious illness, ridicule from Europeans, some of whose behaviour seriously undermined their message, and contacts whose initial interest melted away when they understood the call to holiness. They did meet enslaved people who were Christians, which was a great encouragement, as well as unexpected support from some colonisers. Most of their contact was with men and there is no mention of Rebecca and her work in their records. Nitschmann left St Thomas after just over a year, as was his plan; his wife and child were waiting for him back at Herrnhut. Dober stayed on for another year, but his work became difficult: a violent slave uprising broke out on a neighbouring island, meaning that plantation owners became

3. Oldendorp, *History of the Mission of the Evangelical Brethren*, 273.

even more hostile to the liberating message of the gospel. Dober became ill, and a famine affected the whole of the island. After months of seeking God's will, Dober reluctantly decided to leave his three converts and the ongoing work to others and return to Europe. The new team of three missionaries, however, all died within their first two months of arriving on the Island, the result of a prolonged voyage and fever. The first Moravian mission to St Thomas had lasted just two years.

Partnership in service

Friedrich Martin was a charismatic man, who was described as having 'a fiery spirit and sound common sense'. He had become convinced that it was Jesus Christ himself, not any human being, who 'initiates faith and brings it to its fulfilment' and so yearned to present Christ to new people.[4] Three years after the team of missionaries had died, Martin and two other German Moravians arrived on St Thomas. They travelled to the Caribbean forewarned about the difficulties of the work and environment by Dober, and so were able to make a wise beginning. Martin talked to enslaved people and handed out Bibles wherever possible. A few were interested in his teaching, and knowing the appeal of literacy to the enslaved, Martin began teaching any who were allowed (and some who weren't) to creep away after a long hard day. There, in an overcrowded, stuffy room in his house, the Bible was not only deciphered but discussed, and its revolutionary passages about freedom, suffering and mercy were explored. In a short time, and with great joy, Martin was able to baptise three men.

4. Oldendorp, *History of the Mission of the Evangelical Brethren*, 306.

There was plenty of opposition to this baby church. Some of those who attempted to attend were whipped and beaten; for these people the teaching of 1 Peter 2 about bearing up under unjust persecution and imitating Christ in his sufferings, were hard but precious lessons. And as the church grew, with women as well as men showing spiritual hunger, Friedrich Martin realised he needed more help.

Rebecca was just the person. Another Moravian who visited Martin and met Rebecca in 1736, wrote home about this eighteen-year-old, saying, 'She is well versed in the Scriptures and could be a worker ... She is free, behaves like a white, and avoids all bad company. The [black] women have great trust in her, and she makes a special effort to instruct them. But she has much work to do, because she is in service to a Master and carries the keys of the entire household. She is a trustworthy woman.'[5]

The positive description of her as behaving 'like a white' makes uncomfortable reading, betraying the dominant racist attitudes of the time. Though the Moravians firmly believed in the equality of all people before God, they didn't believe in the equality of all cultures or manners. For them, European culture, which had been shaped by Christianity, was superior to the culture of the African diaspora despite the fact that many of the habits of white people were morally neutral, such as their taste in music and dress, or even just plain sinful, such as their ideas of racial superiority. Still, Rebecca's zeal stands out. The Moravians were realising that God had gifted her and called her

5. Quoted by Jon F. Sensbach, *Rebecca's Revival* (Harvard University Press, Cambridge, Mass., 2005), 67.

to further his work on the island. Christ's compassion for the oppressed was being displayed in Rebecca's salvation and in her service to those trapped and burdened by slavery.

The suggestion that 'she could be a worker' in this letter shows us not just how remarkable Rebecca was, but also, as how seriously the Moravian church took the needs, and the giftedness, of women. 'Worker' was the name given to a Ministry Assistant with particular, clearly identified responsibilities. While the head of the movement was Count Nikolaus Zinzendorf himself and the preachers in local gatherings were male, their system of classes, or Bible Studies, organised by sex and sometimes by life stage, meant that women taught and discipled each other. The Moravian vision of church life was that each person had their own tale to tell of the Lord's goodness and a role to play in the life of the church, whether it was in mission, practical service or prayer. Before she was twenty years old, Rebecca was serving as a 'worker'. She was the first black woman, and among the first generation of women anywhere, to be officially set aside for service in the Protestant church.

St Thomas is just 32 square miles, long and thin, and divided by a rough mountain spine. In the eighteenth century, there were two paths which allowed people to get around. In the dark after work was finished or on a Sunday or Saturday afternoon, enslaved people could travel these steep routes, often barefoot, to see friends or visit a child or spouse. Many streamed to St Thomas's small port town on Sundays to sell a few sweet potatoes or calabash, or a basket they'd made. After nine at night, however, any found walking could be imprisoned or even beaten. Sometimes, plantation owners would display severed body parts – a hand or even a head – along the way to deter anyone who thought they could rebel. Owners were conscious of some small bands of runaway slaves hiding on the mountainsides, and the memory of armed slave uprisings on other nearby islands lingered in the minds of the white population. You might be able to walk a few miles, these grisly signs said, but you're not really free at all.

Travelling on these fearsome paths was the only way for Rebecca to get about for her mission work. Once her housekeeping tasks were done for the day and those on the plantations had finished their work, Rebecca would gather up her skirts and trek along the path to sit in a slave village, really no more than a cluster of huts, just downwind from the overseer's house. Round the fire there would be conversation, teaching and songs of worship. She taught some women to read and, as she did so, explained Bible passages. She offered comfort and counsel, but most of all the offer of forgiveness and the hope of heavenly freedom. On Sundays, some went to the church meeting in Martin's school room. Rebecca would be there to worship and talk, and lead classes for women.

Being able to speak the same language as the slaves as well as the Dutch Creole spoken by planters was a massive benefit for Rebecca. She knew too, far better than Martin and the other German missionaries, not only how slaves lived but also what they believed. Many transported from West Africa held on to their faith in both the spirits of ancestors and divine spirits, some of whom were remote and others who were near. For some these, beliefs were mixed with Catholic teaching passed on in more recent generations. Spirits could be pleased or angered, and it was important that certain rituals and ceremonies take place to secure their favour. There was dancing and drumming at night in the woods and complex funeral rituals; sacred objects were treasured and offerings of food made. At the centre of all this, in each plantation was the Obeah, the 'witch doctor', who treated the sick and communicated with the spiritual world.

To speak of Jesus in this society didn't just risk stirring up the anger of white colonisers. It could also be opposed by the enslaved workers, savagely torn from their homes and trying to cling on to their African identity. The fact that Rebecca had herself been snatched from her mother's home as a child must have helped her understand their fears. And perhaps her message was accepted more willingly because Rebecca was prepared to sit down alongside those who had so little, though she herself had gained freedom. In her presence they could see something of 'the grace of our Lord Jesus Christ, that though he was rich, yet for your sake he became poor, so that you through his poverty might become rich' (2 Corinthians 8:9). It was her own experience of Christ's compassion and the example of his life that led Rebecca to go out to the poorest. In one of her few letters, written in 1737, she bursts out in prayer, 'O, help me to praise him, who has pulled me out of the darkness. I will take up his cross with all my heart and follow the example of his poor life.'[6]

For women who had been kidnapped from their homes or born into servitude, turning to Christ brought joy, as they discovered their status in the eyes of God. Made in his image and saved at the cost of his Son, they were loved so deeply. They had a new identity, as servants of a loving King and a new

6. Quoted by Sensbach, *Rebecca's Revival*, 63.

family, which wasn't determined by colour, race or tribe. Their new book, the Bible, told stories of liberation from slavery and the hope of a promised land of freedom. It provided songs of lament through which they could voice their griefs, longing and assurance; they could cry both, 'How long, Lord?' and, 'I will sing the Lord's praise, for he has been good to me' (Psalm 13:1, 6). Ahead of them was the certainty of heaven where there would be no more pain or tears. Faith also brought practical questions for these abused women who were pressured to have sex or forcibly parted from their husbands. Along with Martin, Rebecca had to think through hard questions about living as a Christian while being enslaved, trying to tease out how to apply the Bible in a non-European context, so she could offer comfort and wisdom to her little bands of believers.

Very quickly the church grew. On one estate, for example, it began with just one slave, Matamba, who in 1737 had an extraordinary dream while still on the passage across the Atlantic that white men would come to help and teach him. He heard about Martin's preaching and in time became a Christian. Not long after this, he himself was preaching. A female slave from the same estate joined Matamba in baptism. A year later, fourteen more professed faith, the year after, twenty-two were baptised. In 1739, eighty enslaved workers from Matamba's estate were part of the church. What happened in one small plantation was happening elsewhere, too. A revival was taking place all over the island, and sixty per cent of these new Christians were women.

With this rapid growth, the mission strategy was refined and Rebecca's role developed. They now aimed to reach out to two people on an estate or in a village, and then train these converts to reach others. New converts were arranged into small single-sex 'bands' for prayer and encouragement. It seems that Africans from different tribal groups were deliberately put together so that any existing ethnic or cultural rivalries could be overcome. Rebecca became part of a team of freed and enslaved people, most of them men, assisting and advising Martin. But more help was needed. New missionaries arrived from Germany to partner with Martin and Rebecca. Rebecca had the joy of serving alongside Veronica, the wife of one of the new Moravian workers. Taking new leaders aside for more in-depth teaching, Veronica and Rebecca were urgently trying to shape more 'Rebeccas' who would follow them in the work, and perhaps even carry on the mission without them. Neither could have known how important this was to be, in light of the catastrophe which lay ahead.

A missionary marriage

Marriage was important to Moravians. They placed a big emphasis on Christ as the loving bridegroom of the church; marriage was a holy preparation for the ultimate union of believers with their Saviour. It wasn't just about having children or companionship, and certainly not about a private romance, but about fighting together for personal holiness and to spread the message of the gospel. These were only some of the reasons why, in 1738, Martin thought it might be a good idea for the twenty-year-old Rebecca to be married. He explained to church leaders back in Herrnhut that it would help her ministry among the enslaved women, most of whom were married. She'd be able to empathise with them. But also, he thought, it would mean no one could spread rumours about her relationships with the male missionaries either.

What Rebecca thought about the idea we can only guess from her responses to different suitors. Moravian marriages were a public matter and had to be arranged with the church authorities, so a rather slow process involving letters sent back and forth across the Atlantic began. But the man and woman involved also had their say; first one of the three German ministers on the island asked Martin if a marriage between him and Rebecca could be arranged. Martin suggested it to Rebecca, but she point-blank refused. Timothy was worldly and confused, she said, so she'd have none of it. Rebecca wanted partnership with a spiritual equal.

Martin thought that the other unmarried German, Matthaus Freundlich, might be a better option and so began negotiating between the two and the Moravian hierarchy. Rebecca seems to have been reluctant: Martin wrote that she had to be asked several times 'in part from bashfulness, in part because she felt herself too lowly'.[7] Maybe marriage itself was unappealing. It could have been that the thought of being married to a European was overwhelming, threatening her African identity. The prospect of being tied down in a new way, losing some of the freedom she had only just found, or the danger of childbirth, may have made her hesitate. Perhaps she just wasn't particularly attracted to Matthaus. In the end, she agreed: 'not my own, but my Saviour's will be done'.[8] Hardly the response many bridegrooms would be looking for, and a not too subtle hint that Rebecca saw this union as part of her Christian obedience rather than the fulfilment of a heart desire.

7. Sensbach, *Rebecca's Revival*, 104.

8. Sensbach, *Rebecca's Revival*, 104.

The marriage took place late after classes one day in March 1738, probably in Martin's house. There were prayers, promises and a symbolic joining of hands over which Martin officiated. And with not just the approval of her employers, but also their generous and practical gifts, Rebecca moved to the mission house. Now she was a housekeeper, not for a wealthy family but for three men who struggled for income. She also became a foster mother to nine children who had been taken in by the missionaries. Although no longer in paid employment, her days must have felt in some ways similar to those of her single life. There was the exhausting round of cooking, cleaning, teaching and counselling, though now with the addition of little bodies to clothe and feed, to worry about and comfort. Ill and hungry people could turn up at the door hoping for food and words of comfort. No wonder the men had been keen on a marriage taking place; they must have had domestic help before Rebecca's arrival, but now they had a sister in Christ, a trusted co-worker and an experienced housekeeper to help them at home as well as in the outside ministry.

Two extraordinary events followed Rebecca's marriage. One was the decision of Martin to buy a plantation, complete with slaves. We might find this impossible to understand, but for the Moravians, stretched to their limit with pastoral and evangelistic work, while toiling hard to earn enough to buy food and clothes, never mind Bibles and other things they needed for ministry, it felt a logical step. Although this is no justification for what they did, slavery was so engrained in their culture and experience that while a long-term aim might have been to get rid of it, in the short-term they accepted it. Owning a plantation would bring in income and provide them with a base for ministry. Land and buildings would be much better than a cramped town house. They would be out of the small port town and much closer to the hundreds they were already serving. To take ownership of slaves would be to provide them with a better life than in a regular plantation and to share the gospel with many more people. Certainly, we know that quite a few mission organisations purchased estates and on them Europeans and Africans often worked side by side harvesting crops and processing food. In this model, inevitably productivity rates were lower, as the enslaved were given more time off. What Rebecca thought about all of this, and whether she felt the ends justified the means, we will never know. She barely would have had time to reflect, however, before the next extraordinary event in her life occurred. Just a few months after the move, Rebecca, Matthaus and Martin were arrested and imprisoned in the Island's fort.

3

Change and Crisis

The waves of enslaved people who were learning to read and gathering at crowded meetings discussing Christian freedom and new life was making plantation owners scared. In their fine houses at a distance from the clusters of huts and dusty marketplaces, and outnumbered four to one, they were terrified of uprisings. The missionaries and the God they worshipped were a competing authority – slaves were willing to disobey their owners so that they could honour God – and so missionaries and converts had to be stopped.

First came an attack on Rebecca and Matthaus's marriage. Martin, it was claimed, lacked authority to officiate at marriages, baptisms or the Lord's Supper, despite the fact that the Danish King himself had granted the Moravians permission to work on the island. Martin was charged with illegally performing these services and forbidden from any religious activity except preaching. Rebecca and Matthaus were charged with fornication, following the logic that if their marriage ceremony wasn't lawful, then their relationship was a scandalous sexual sin. They weren't thrown in jail at this stage, but they were left not knowing whether they could carry on their work. There's a huge and sad irony here, of course. Some masters raped their slaves and tolerated slaves living in polygamous relationships. They broke up families when they bought and sold slaves, but a consensual Christian marriage was outlawed.

Martin wrote letter after letter, begging the Danish King who had supported the mission from its outset to intervene. The Governor wrote to his seniors in Denmark too, asking for advice. But ships were slow, and while everyone was waiting for a response, the legal attacks took on another form. First, Rebecca, Matthaus and Martin were accused of being accomplices in a robbery. The charges made little sense, but that didn't stop numerous draining court appearances. Day after day they had to turn up in the intimidating panelled court room and answer questions. What made everything more difficult was that the Moravians refused to take an oath. Like other non-conformists of the time, they believed that Matthew 5:33-37 prohibited swearing an oath in court. It was enough to tell the truth, they thought. In court accounts of the trials, you can sense the understandable frustration of the magistrates at what looked like simple stubbornness but also the dignity and integrity of the missionaries. After many agonising twists and turns, all charges were thrown out, but then the marriage question was raised again. Finally in October 1738, just seven months after Rebecca and Matthaus's wedding, the three missionaries were thrown in jail because they didn't have funds to pay a fine. The plantation owners thought they had got what they wanted.

For a month, the three were stuck in a cell underneath the fort. Unlike imprisoned slaves, they did have some daylight through a small window, but that was about all. Worn down by months of legal wrangling they were now on their own. Roasting hot by day and freezing at night, with nothing to sleep on, this was no rest. But it was in many ways what they had longed for. These three workers had joined the company of heroes they had heard of for so many years; they were like Peter and Paul and the great martyrs who had suffered for their faith.

Outside the fort, crowds of supporters gathered to sing and pray. Some brought food and wine, facing severe punishments from their owners for doing so. Inside, Rebecca, Matthaus and Martin sang and prayed too, clinging on to God's promise that he would uphold them. They knew what Peter taught when he instructed Christians to bear up under persecution just as Christ did. They also knew that if they gave up, the effect on the church would be disastrous, so they stood their ground.

The slave-owners' plans backfired as sympathy for the imprisoned grew. The missionaries stuck to their word. Black male co-workers, with Martin's encouragement, had taken up the preaching and teaching duties. New converts were baptised, and over the winter of the Freundlich's imprisonment, even while increasingly harsh treatment was being handed out to slaves who tried to attend meetings, 200 believers were added to the church. On an Island where the black population numbered around 3,500, this would have been a really noticeable movement. Since Martin arrived under two years before, perhaps ten per cent of the enslaved people were now professing faith.

This wonderful news didn't necessarily make life in the cell any easier. The brutal environment made first Martin, and then the others, ill. He was allowed out to recover, but Matthaus and Rebecca were left inside. The authorities doubled the fine they were demanding for the 'false marriage', then tripled it and kept bringing the three to court to face more questions and charges. Finally, after fourteen weeks in the damp and dark room, a verdict was announced. As they couldn't pay the fine, Rebecca must become a slave again and Matthaus must return to Europe where he would most certainly face prison. This was perhaps just what Rebecca had feared; when white people were in charge, a black person could never really be free.

An extraordinary arrival

God works in extraordinary ways. What happened next would seem implausible if written in a novel. While desperate letters were being sent on the slow voyage across the Atlantic and then overland to Germany and Denmark, pleading for royal or religious intervention. Count Nikolaus Zinzendorf was travelling in the opposite direction. Inspired by the regular reports which the missionaries had sent, he wanted to see the revival on St Thomas for himself and so had set sail. He arrived on shore completely unaware of the injustice his workers were suffering and walked right into the storm.

'Where are the brothers?' he asked as soon as he disembarked. He received the reply, 'In prison.' Martin's illness meant he was under a kind of house arrest, while Rebecca and Matthaus, having received their final sentence, were in the fort waiting for it to be carried out. Nikolaus wasted no time. His status trumped that even of the island's Governor. A nobleman with connections to the Danish monarch was more important that a colonial administrator. He called on the prisoners and the Governor called on him. After fifteen weeks of imprisonment and seven court appearances, it only took Nikolaus a few conversations to negotiate a release, showing how arbitrary and corrupt the court's actions had been.

Rebecca was overjoyed. She wrote to Christian sisters in Germany that the Count was the 'key' the Lord had used to open the prison door.[1] This was a miracle, she said. The Lord had proven himself faithful; she had known 'sweetness' in prison, and she had been given the opportunity to share this with hundreds of others, and now she was free. Her faith had not been ground down by her trials but strengthened. And now the once enslaved and imprisoned woman, with the fumes of the cell still clinging to her simple clothes, met the noble Count. Rebecca had been a star of Martin's regular reports and she, of course, had heard of the head of the church; how they must have enjoyed sharing their stories. He didn't stay on the island long, however. Having arrived like a whirlwind, he spent a brief time with the church worshipping and offering the workers advice, then he vanished again. After he left, persecution was stirred once more. The plantation owners had been shamed by Nikolaus's intervention, and the church was growing even more than before, so fury and fear poured out. White men burst into prayer meetings with weapons; slaves were beaten and the missionaries, Rebecca included, were threatened. It must have been completely exhausting, especially for the now pregnant Rebecca.

Her child, Anna Maria, was born ten or so months after the escape from prison, in late 1739, when Rebecca was still only about twenty-one. Neither pregnancy nor motherhood seem to have slowed Rebecca down. Tying the baby to her back, she

1. Quoted in Sensbach, *Rebecca's Revival*, 131.

continued to care for other children in her home, instruct the female assistants and visit slaves in their own huts. Though the leadership team had grown, with a new German couple as well as more enslaved people serving, she was still at the heart of the mission.

In November 1741, Rebecca and Matthaus chose to leave St Thomas and travel to Germany. Burnt out and run down, it was an obvious choice for Matthaus. The opportunity to reconnect with family and homeland must have seemed very welcome. For both of them, the enforced stillness of a month-long passage across the Atlantic would have been the only way to escape their relentless care-giving roles. This must have been the first break Rebecca had experienced in her life. What was there to do on board but care for Anna Maria, read her Bible and pray? What lay ahead must have driven her prayers. She was journeying into the unknown, away from the only type of society she had ever known, away from people who looked like her, and to a land where she would always be seen as an alien. Still, they were going to the Count and to the community of grace she had heard so much about, where there was no threat of violence and where they could be free to worship.

A new life in a new community

Herrnhaag (meaning the Lord's Grove), the Freundlich family's destination, was an extraordinary place. This was the second settlement created by the Moravians, not far from Herrnhut on Count Zinzendorf's original estates, now close to the border with the Czech Republic. It had elegant purpose-built buildings, which aimed to represent the heavenly Jerusalem described in Revelation, with twelve gates and a central well, a symbol of the river of life. It was called a 'Mother', with the community conscious of its role as bride of Christ. The reason for the establishment of a new centre, however, was not growth or enlarged vision, but another kind of persecution. Although Nikolaus had always envisaged that the Moravians would be a group within the Lutheran Church, and had been ordained as a Lutheran pastor to prove this, by 1736 state authorities had banished him and his community from his estates. Possibly correctly, they doubted he held to the confessions of the established church. Nikolaus's focus had always been on forms of holiness and his priority had been the pursuit of unity, not doctrine. The group's name, after all, was 'The Unity of the Brethren'.

At Herrnhaag, as at Herrnhut, the community was secluded from the world and financially self-supporting. There was a pattern of daily worship and lengthy prayer vigils. The wounds of Christ were a focus for passionate devotion and communion was celebrated as a 'love feast', with regular ceremonies of foot washing. Today we might look on these practices and see something cult-like in their intensity, questioning the aspects of their theology which interpreted union with Christ in an almost material way. Certainly, in the mid-1740s, when Nikolaus was absent from the community some concerning excesses arose. Yet, there was no doubt that in this world Christ's work on the cross was central and faith meant total devotion to him. Men and women – even those who were married – lived in separate quarters divided according to age and marital status. Children were cared for on site in dormitories where they were educated and taught the Scriptures.

Whilst this structure might seem to us unnatural and even oppressive, there were some benefits. The separation of the sexes meant that women, as well as men, were actively encouraged to take on leadership within their groups, or 'choirs'. And in other Moravian centres established in the 1740s, although the living arrangements weren't always replicated, the opportunities for service were. The role of Assistant which Rebecca had on St Thomas was one of several positions open to the residents of Herrnhaag. Almost as in a convent, female teachers and spiritual leaders were set aside to train and support other girls and women. Anna Nitschmann (1715-1760), daughter of David Nitschmann who had briefly served on St Thomas, stood out as 'Chief Elderess'. From her late teens she had overall charge of the women's spiritual development and contributed to the discussions of the senior male leaders. We're told that she also travelled on a 'preaching tour', though what this means isn't quite clear and we've no evidence that she preached regularly to mixed congregations. The fledgling Moravian Church seems to have been the first Protestant group where women who were neither rich nor married to influential men had their contributions to church life actively encouraged and formally acknowledged.

Among the Moravians, a practice of recording autobiographies grew up, which would become a hallmark of the evangelical revival in Britain and beyond. Each individual's conversion and growth in grace was entered into the narrative of the community. Many were even finished off by others, so we can now read all about the childhoods, working lives and even deaths of many eighteenth-century women. The pietist belief in the importance of the inner life of the believer meant that women's faith, labour and self-understanding were treasured. We read in these narratives about conviction of sin, relationships with parents, repentance, work, marriage, spiritual joy and grief; they are a fascinating depiction of what faith meant for women.

How Rebecca felt about this new world isn't recorded. She arrived in May 1742, aged still only twenty-four. The journey had lasted six months and with all probability she was overwhelmed. The young woman who left St Thomas a wife, arrived at her destination a widow. After the slow sea crossing, when the travellers were making their way through Germany and were only a few days away from the Moravian community at Marienborn, Matthaus suddenly became ill. Within twenty-four hours he was dead.

Rebecca must have been in deep shock. Her husband was gone and she was in an alien land among strangers. Germany must have been bewildering in its newness. Its food and weather no doubt seemed drab, and the scale of the austere red-roofed buildings, housing many hundreds of believers, quite extraordinary when compared to the huts of slaves and even the colonial estates. Still, the church's intense communal life provided comfort. Some of their routines were familiar to her from those the Moravian missionaries had brought to the Caribbean. Rebecca was used to living at close quarters with other Christians and being housed with other widows probably allowed her opportunity to grieve. Rebecca had picked up some German as well as Danish on St Thomas, so she could communicate. Little Anna Maria was with her and she was out of the turbulence and intensity of ministry. These were perhaps blessings in a hard time of grief.

Waiting for her at Herrnhaag were old friends. Maria and Andreas, enslaved Africans from St Thomas, had worked alongside Rebecca and been purchased by Moravians in order to be liberated. They'd arrived in Herrnhaag a few years before

Rebecca, married and joined the increasing group of 'first fruits', converts from missionary work further afield. This group consisted of others from the Caribbean, a man from Sri Lanka; a 'Tartar' from somewhere in Central Asia; indigenous Americans, as well as people from Greenland, Estonia and England. Although perhaps there was an unhealthy fascination with these non-Europeans, their voices were listened to. When the annual Synod of the Brethren was gathered – a kind of AGM for the movement – it was an international event, with Rebecca chosen in the year after her arrival to represent St Thomas.

Though she must have been, at least at first, something of a celebrity, the structures of daily life may well have helped Rebecca to fit in. She wore the standard clothing of the community: a neat white bonnet and blouse over which a dark bodice was laced, with bright ribbons lacing these to indicate life stage or choir. It didn't take her long to be called to serve as a Deaconess, meaning that, alongside male Deacons, she helped preachers in all kinds of duties and took part in serving communion. We can see that she took her place in the prayer life of the community as her name appears on the rotas for the regular cycles of twenty-four-hour prayer.

While the routines of Herrnhaag and Rebecca's devoted involvement continued, she suffered yet more grief and change. Two years after her arrival, her little daughter died and two years after that she married again. As before, this was no sentimental romance. Marriage was arranged by the Elders of the community, though both participants had freedom to accept or reject the proposal. The self-control and grace Rebecca required in this situation must have been immense. She was twenty-eight years old and had already experienced so much. The turbulence and losses had forced her to cling to Christ, but surely not without internal struggle. She was living out the truths of Romans 5:3-6, finding that suffering produces perseverance, character and hope, through the work of the Spirit and the knowledge of Christ.

Full circle

It is easy to see why Christian Protten was chosen for Rebecca. He had been born on the Gold Coast, Rebecca's mother's homeland. He was the son of a Danish sailor and a tribal leader's daughter. We're told that his parents had married, though what happened to his father, we don't know. Christian had been educated by a European believer and aged eleven his abilities marked him out. He had been taken away from his mother to travel to Copenhagen where he was baptised and spent years studying, including at a university. He was restless, however, and seems to have felt keenly his ambiguous position as a man of dual heritage in Europe. Though free, he felt that he had been taken from his people unfairly and not given the same opportunities as a white man. Among Moravians in Germany, he found a kind of home and some degree of peace, though it wasn't to last long and he gladly took an opportunity to return to the Gold Coast as a missionary. After four difficult years he was recalled to Herrnhaag, arriving there just before Rebecca's traumatic entry into the community.

These experiences of wandering and disappointment continued into married life. Four years after their wedding, celebrated en masse with other Moravian couples, the Prottens had a daughter, but from birth she was weak and very sadly died when she was nearly four years old. Perhaps this grief was too much for Christian on top of his other frustrations; at times a heavy drinker he seems to have got into conflict with church leaders. It might have seemed a relief when in 1756, ten years after their marriage, he went back to the Gold Coast on his own in an attempt to restart his earlier work, leaving Rebecca to continue with her mentoring, teaching and caring in the place which had become her home. A letter that exists from this period shows her great tenderness and care for her husband so many miles away as she encourages him:

> *You know well that I love you and I never will forget it. That I promise, but, poor me, what will your poor heart do in these times? Turn to Him, who has everything.*[2]

Christian did trust his Saviour but struggled as he faced frustration and isolation in everything he attempted. His desire was to establish a mission station on the coast which could be a launch pad for inland outreach, but this was resisted by the authorities, and they instead urged him to teach the growing number of children who, like him, had been fathered by European traders. Christian did set up a school which he wanted to base in a black village, but again this plan was ruled out. The enterprise had instead to be conducted in the symbol of colonial exploitation, Fort Christiansborg, with its slave dungeons and military defences. Keeping his concern for reaching African people alive, Christian researched indigenous religions and prepared an introduction to the Fante and Ga languages. Still, this stay ended in in shame when after five years a child died

2. Quoted by Sensbach, *Rebecca's Revival*, 212.

under his watch. He cried out in a letter, 'I have made a mess of everything.'[3] In 1762, Christian returned to Germany and to his wife of sixteen years, exhausted and without funds. He'd even walked the last 300 miles from Copenhagen to the re-established centre at Herrnhut, where Rebecca was now based.

What must Rebecca have felt when her husband returned home? Her joy at the reunion may well have been mixed with apprehension about what it might mean and even dismay at the inevitable disruption to her orderly life. His arrival certainly brought upheaval, as no sooner had the reunion taken place, plans for a return to Africa began. Christian clearly didn't feel he fitted in within the constrained routines of the community, and he was still not on easy terms with the leaders. Getting these plans underway took two years as the couple shuttled between Moravian groups across the Netherlands, Germany and even Britain as well as the Danish Court, seeking funds and support. Christian had to justify his intentions with detailed written reports for the King, as Christiansborg (now Ghana's capital, Accra), where they were headed was a Danish colonial outpost. He also had to prove that he was reliable to Moravian congregations, from which he was begging financial support. It seems that each only gave him their loose change, intensifying his pain and possibly causing him to drink again. His heart was still set on preaching Christ, but he was a broken, wounded man.

The events of the Prottens' arrival on the Gold Coast now seem symbolic of their ministry. In 1764, having disembarked from the ship which had brought them from Europe, they boarded a boat which would take them through the surf to the shore. This

3. Quoted by Sensbach, *Rebecca's Revival*, 208.

capsized and all their belongings were lost. Documents, books, clothes, money and any precious reminders of Rebecca's two lost daughters and past friends were washed away in the Atlantic waves. There was not even a means of proving who they were to the suspicious colonial authorities, and a stressful exchange of letters between the Danish Court and the local Governor had to ensue before the couple were accepted as residents. Christiansborg's fort was the seat of Danish rule, but around this intimidating structure were the inns for European traders and homes of African merchants. People of different tribal and racial backgrounds mixed together, competing for power and wealth, whilst captured men and women waited in dark cells to be shipped across the ocean. Rebecca faced starting again in this unknown place, this time with no material goods and a troubled, struggling husband. Away from a Christian community where she had status and authority, Rebecca was now in a centre of racial oppression, the very one where her mother had been enslaved. She and Christian, literate arrivals from Europe, were in an ambiguous position. Both of their fathers had been involved in the system of slavery and they were now dependent on the good will of people who practised this trade. No wonder Christian was troubled.

Their heart's desire was to reach black Africans with the gospel. Christian longed to travel into the interior, away from the trading of the coast, and preach to the Ga people. This wasn't allowed, presumably for the same reasons that many plantation owners disliked the gospel being preached to those they enslaved. What they were permitted to do, instead, was to run a school for children of dual heritage, those who had been born, like them, as a result of the complex and most often unequal relationships between Europeans and Africans. Rebecca had charge of the girls, and her remit was to train them in skills which would earn them a living, such as sewing and housekeeping, as well as instruct them in the Christian faith. It is hard to imagine that she didn't also teach them to read and write and share with them all she knew personally of God's tender care. Maybe Rebecca felt transported back to her own early years when she was taught how to read the Scriptures, discovered Christ and received her freedom. She had faced the temptation to exploit her position to be complicit in the slave business, as a go-between for the European masters. Now she was caring for children who were in the same difficult position. How she must have sympathised with them. She and Christian were equipping these children out of their own painful experience for the real hardships and pain of life in a racially divided world, and must have impressed on their pupils the love of a God who welcomes the fatherless and has compassion on the stranger. It wasn't what they had planned to do, but it was a task both had been equipped by God for.

This shared service lasted four years until Christian died. Rebecca was fifty-one, twice widowed and twice bereaved of children. Letters tell us that she was no longer able to serve; she was worn out and prematurely aged, and so a pension was granted to her by the Danish authorities who ran the port. After a few years her Moravian leaders in Germany suggested that she board a slave ship and return to St Thomas, perhaps the place which could best be described as home, but it is easy to understand why she turned this down. She was too frail for the arduous journey, and it had been thirty years since she had set foot in the Caribbean. No one seemed to have questioned the difficulty for her of being a free guest on a ship bearing dozens of men, women and children to a life of unremitting hard labour and bondage, but surely this was another reason not to go.

The remainder of Rebecca's years were spent in great obscurity. She was still well known enough for her death in 1780, about ten years after her husband's, to be noted in Moravian records. Her legacy didn't remain a footnote, though; while she and Christian were teaching the next generation in Christiansborg, a Moravian missionary back on St Thomas was composing a 3,000-page history of the church's life on the island. That today we know so much of Rebecca's story is down to his efforts.

Through this book, Rebecca's ministry was to have a significant yet unforeseen impact. The testimony of enslaved men and women who had turned to Christ and lived lives which were modest and pious was crucial in the campaign against the trade in people. Rebecca's role in the Christian awakening on St Thomas, which brought the immediate spiritual emancipation of hundreds, had political reverberations leading to the physical emancipation of many more. And even today, the church on the island founded through Rebecca's ministry and once filled with enslaved people, resounds with the praise of their liberated descendants. Rebecca's story is a powerful reminder of God's economy. Ministry is Christ-shaped. Just as his Son took on the form of a servant, to bring life to us, so he uses the weak and despised, the servants and enslaved, to carry his message of life to the world. Rebecca's life asks us whether we are ready to listen to the weak and to embrace hardship ourselves; it asks us whether we are ready, as Rebecca was, to be servants of all.

A Partner in the Fight

HANNAH MORE,

1745-1833

4

The Girl Who Knew Her Mind

Hannah More's life could not have been more different from that of Rebecca Protten. If Rebecca's portrait shows a reserved woman, plainly dressed, pictures of Hannah reveal a fashionable, confident individual. Despite this self-assurance, however, Hannah didn't travel outside the borders of her native land and always lived close to family members. She didn't marry and she had no children. She was a life-long, devoted member of the Church of England and was instinctively conservative in nearly everything she did. Hannah ended her days a well-off and well-known figure, with connections to powerful politicians, aristocrats and bishops. These two women, with such different stories, still have much in common. Both were educators and evangelists; both were connected, though in very different ways, with slavery; and above all, both loved Christ and served him with great courage.

Although their lives overlapped, the setting they were born into was hugely different too. Hannah was born in 1745 near Bristol, in the west of England twenty-seven years after Rebecca's mother gave birth in Antigua. While few women in England made it to school, and none had the vote, literacy rates were increasing. At around the time of Hannah's birth, thirty per cent of women could read and write, and this had crept up to around fifty per cent by the time she died eighty-eight years later, getting closer to the male rate of sixty per cent. Some women were highly educated and had some influence. Elizabeth Carter and Elizabeth Montagu, contemporaries of Hannah More, and the earlier figure of Mary Astell, were serious writers and Christian believers. Encouraged by their fathers and their church leaders to learn and use their natural gifting, each received tutoring in subjects that were usually reserved for boys: classical languages, maths and some philosophy. Unlike Hannah, though, they came from well-to-do backgrounds.

Hannah was born in a school-teacher's cottage, just after the arrival of Rebecca Protten in Germany. Hers was a close and happy family, and as in many families, their secrets and shame were hidden away. For nearly two hundred years biographies of Hannah More have told the story that her father, Jacob More, was born into minor gentry, educated in a grammar school, missed out on inheriting land in Norwich and lost his collection of books at sea. This all went to explain how he ended up master of a tiny charity school at the other side of the country. Recent research reveals that at least some of this isn't true; somebody somewhere was covering up.

It turns out that Jacob More worked as a fairly low-level tax official in Bristol and then as a kind of farm manager where, when he was thirty-five, he married sixteen-year-old Grace Lynch, Hannah's mother. At about this time he lost his job, perhaps because he was in disgrace due to getting Grace pregnant before the wedding. A few years later he appears in records as Fishponds Charity School's only teacher.

A close shave with illegitimacy and lower-class roots wouldn't have helped Hannah and her sisters as they set up a business providing a refined education for young ladies, yet their background wasn't out of the ordinary. In this period about a third of brides were pregnant on their wedding day and illegitimacy didn't necessarily make someone disreputable. There was an expectation that men would provide for the children they fathered, either by marrying their sweethearts or providing a form of financial child support. The future King William IV lived happily for ten years with Mrs Jordan, a well-known actress in the 1770s. She already had four illegitimate children by two other fathers and bore the prince ten children, several of whom married into the nobility. She wasn't considered decent enough to become Queen but she certainly wasn't seen as improper. Just as now, education, ambition and the right connections could transform a person's social status, and sexual conventions were fairly flexible, at least in the working and upper classes.

Hannah's family might not have been at the bottom of the social pile, but they weren't at all wealthy. Her father's work can't have been very inspiring, providing the basics in literacy and numeracy for energetic village boys, but the position was steady. The house was small, consisting of a couple of rooms downstairs adjoining the school room and a couple upstairs. Her biographers all tell stories about the games Hannah played, turning over school desks to make a pretend carriage to travel to London and collecting scraps of paper to write stories. Even as a small child in a busy household, Hannah was a born leader, with a voracious desire for experience and confidence in her own voice. She learned to write from her mother and taught herself to read at a very early age. Jacob's clearly sharp mind found its outlet in his daughters' education. They were all keen to learn, but Hannah, fourth of the five girls, seems to have been the most ambitious and eager of them all. She was the only one her father taught Latin and mathematics.

Maybe Hannah's parents had strong views about female education, but more certainly, financial survival was a key reason why the girls were educated. A schoolmaster's wage was certainly not enough to provide for five grown daughters, and there was no son to go out into the world and find a fortune. Most women, apart from the very wealthy, married in their late twenties and before this they worked, handing over some of their small pay to the family. The range of options was narrow. It would have felt degrading for a school master's daughters to become domestic servants or seamstresses, even though the More girls would have grown up doing their fair share of household chores. So, their choices were: governess, school-teacher, shop owner or perhaps senior housekeeper. Not the most exciting possibilities for teenagers, but at least they might provide the possibility of freedom outside of the family home. The More sisters chose to take advantage of a new phenomenon: schools for girls.

At the age Rebecca Protten was still enslaved, doing long days of domestic work, Hannah More was being taught in her sisters' school in preparation to become a teacher herself. Mary, the oldest, had left home at the age of twenty with Betty and Sally, advertising the opening of a new school in the local Bristol newspaper. Only Patty, the youngest by five years stayed at home. To proclaim your ability to educate others when you yourself are barely an adult might seem ludicrous today, but it wasn't in 1758. In the Mores' school, girls were taught maths, reading, writing, French, needlework and dancing. It is tempting to read back into this school curriculum Hannah's later convictions about the seriousness of education. Perhaps as the school progressed, and she grew up into her twenties, lessons did become more academic, we just don't know. We do know that thirteen-year-old Hannah learned her lessons alongside these more privileged girls, polishing her French which was one of the prime accomplishments required for polite society. At the same time Hannah somehow taught herself Italian and Spanish as well as taking private lessons in Latin, impressing her teacher with her keen ability, which he said was beyond that of his young male pupils. Although after a few years she took her place alongside her sisters as a teacher, Hannah definitely knew that her future wasn't going to be confined to the schoolroom or even the parlours of the new Bristol chattering classes.

Spreading wings

Away from their village home, the More sisters enjoyed the excitement of living in a rapidly developing city. Bristol was the second port of England and the centre of the slave trade. Luxury goods were unloaded at the docks: chocolate, tobacco, sugar and coffee, all spoils from the business of human trafficking. Other local industries of pottery and glass-making flourished as the middle classes throughout Britain invested in must-have luxury goods. The money being earned financed the building of elegant three and four storey town houses, trips to the spa at Bath just a few miles away, school fees and philanthropy. The sisters benefitted from this boom as their school grew and their own status was secured. The Mores quickly became not just teachers of privileged young women, but guests in their homes as well.

Bristol was flourishing as a cultural centre with this new wealth. As she grew older, Hannah attended public lectures and became an avid theatre goer, sometimes taking pupils to the intimate Theatre Royal, where she could be part of a noisy, excited audience, some concentrating on the play and others wanting to show off their new clothes, ogle the actresses or just see their friends. The theatre in the eighteenth century was an intoxicating place. Where else could you witness love affairs, fighting or death, and come away unscathed, or smell mingled sweat and candle-grease, laugh at risqué jokes or chaotic farce, and still be respectable? At the theatre Hannah wept at tragedies by Shakespeare and giggled at up-to-date comedies, storing up her own ambitions to become a part of this wonderful world.

And everywhere Hannah went, she made friends. While still a teenager she approached an astronomer, James Ferguson, who was giving lectures in the city and received some private lessons from him. She presented a poem to Thomas Sheridan, a famous actor and became his life-long friend. Both these men who were much older than her sought her advice and seemed to have trusted her opinion. There must have been something extraordinary about Hannah that meant she had the self-confidence to approach men in the public eye, and that they paid her such attention. She knew she wanted more than a comfortable life teaching; she wanted attention and intellectual stimulation.

Perhaps more significant that these encounters though, was Hannah's friendship with her neighbour Sir James Stonhouse, another older man who was both a doctor and vicar. He had once rejected Christianity completely and even wrote a pamphlet against the faith, but through the influence of Philip Doddridge, a well-known non-conformist minister, he had turned back to God. Stonhouse had become a friend of the preacher George Whitefield who, along with Charles Wesley and others, had brought the message of justification by faith, forgiveness and free grace, to thousands around Britain and beyond. In the years around Hannah's birth, fields outside Bristol had been filled with crowds of miners, moved to tears by this message, but it hadn't penetrated the More family; in fact, her father was decidedly opposed to it. So while Stonhouse shared conversations and books with Hannah and her sisters and they respected his fatherly care and thoughtful advice, they didn't join with him in his evangelical faith.

Whether the networking was initially motivated by hard-headed ambition or simple enjoyment of male company and curiosity about the world, it is hard to say, but it was used by God later in her life to great good. Even in an age of very distinct and in many ways restricted roles for men and women, mutually beneficial partnership could flourish between them; they didn't exist in completely separate spheres. Still, Hannah had to be very careful in her selection of friends. They were most often older than her and married so that there would be no opportunity for gossip.Visible virtue really mattered to her, but so did inner purity. Hannah had been brought up as a serious church goer.

She avoided card playing on Sundays and was insistent on church attendance, pursuing goodness, but not God, with the same energy that she pursued cultural experience.

When Hannah was only eighteen, she wrote a play for the pupils in the school called *The Search After Happiness* which is really a simple dramatised conversation in verse about contentment. The main character ends the play:

> *CONTENT alone in VIRTUE we can find,*
> *And HAPPINESS exists but in the MIND.*

It's no surprise that this message about the happiness to be found in virtue – not fame or fashion or ignorance – was popular with parents and teachers, though perhaps not the girls themselves. The play is very typical of its time, from the jingling rhyming scheme to the classical references and the rather stoical theme of self-control. Hannah certainly believed in this message, but she also had other motives. The poem includes a spirited argument in defence of female writing, and so it lays out Hannah's confident belief in her own worth and future.

What is particularly interesting about *The Search After Happiness* is the insistence on the intellect, the 'mind'. Hannah emphasises that learning is good, not as an accomplishment to impress others, but as a way to gain contentment and virtue, if pursued with humility. She was striking away from the popular belief that women should be educated simply to make them refined or win husbands and expressing instead a very eighteenth-century optimism about human rationality. In time, this idea would seem insufficient for Hannah and she would discover that something more than effort and logic was needed for human happiness. Eventually the themes and tensions of this, her first published play, would find resolution when she discovered Jesus' power to change lives.

Finding freedom

Hannah may have looked as though she was living a free life in Bristol. She could hide away to write after school hours, venture out into the city for entertainment and enjoy visiting friends in the holidays and evenings. Her more than capable older sisters managed the school, dealing with difficult students and their parents, while turning it into a money-making enterprise, leaving her free of anxiety. In some ways she was a typical younger child, doted on and protected by her siblings. Yet, she was a teacher and part of a family business, tied to a particular place and with many hours taken up in instructing sometimes reluctant pupils. Her status and income were limited. She must have thought that financial security and any kind of fulfilment could only come about through hard work and study. But this was to change.

In 1767, when she was about twenty-two years old Hannah received and accepted a proposal of marriage from William Turner, a gentleman complete with grand house and country estate in the rolling hills outside Bristol. William was the cousin of two of the Mores' pupils who had invited Hannah and a couple of her sisters to his home for a break in the school holidays. William was awed by Hannah's sparkiness and talent. Hannah wasn't classically beautiful; she was plump with long brown ringlets and no special features, except for her intelligent dark eyes and confident smile. This engagement caused real surprise in a day when class connections or looks were the most important attractions. But William was older than Hannah and a quiet man; she must have seemed like a charming whirlwind to him. Whether she felt real love for him is harder to tell; certainly they got on well and she must have appreciated how seriously he took her work. He treated her with great generosity and respect, giving her just what feminists centuries later would say were the essentials for independence. William financed Hannah and set her up a sweet room of her own in the house just for writing. He had some of her poems carved into way markers around his landscaped grounds, where they remain to this day.

In becoming an engaged woman, Hannah had achieved freedom, of a sort. She gave up her teaching role and purchased a trunk full of grand clothes so she could play the part of a leisured gentlewoman. How she must have enjoyed choosing fabrics and trying on the latest styles! No longer did she have to look like a sober school teacher, and now she could indulge her creativity in writing and reading too. William asked for her advice in landscaping his grounds to make them fit the latest picturesque fashion, and she began to host parties at his home, cultivating friendships and setting people at ease. He had found a delightful companion, who could help him feel at ease in his wealth; Hannah had found a level of peace and opportunity she would never have dreamed of in her father's cramped cottage.

But this dream would never be fulfilled. William Turner clearly adored Hannah as a friend, but he couldn't follow through to marriage. Three times over six long years, the wedding was postponed, and on the third repeat in 1773, Hannah's friend James Stonhouse and her sisters intervened. For all the material benefits of being engaged to such an affluent and genteel man, this unresolved situation was humiliating. It had to end. After conversation with her friends, Turner released Hannah from her ties and, what's more, agreed to pay her an annual allowance in recognition of the difficulty caused by this disappointment. Turner remained unmarried for the rest of his life and kept up the financial support, even leaving Hannah a legacy in his will as a sign of his enduring respect. Though this release brought Hannah complete financial and emotional independence, she was deeply upset. Six years is a long time and, for someone who was as concerned about social standing as Hannah, the loss of such a clear, elevated status must have been devastating. She was left adrift. Hannah took a holiday by the sea to bathe her wounds and emerged rejuvenated. Rather than retreat to a dignified, quiet life, she would push forward with her writing career.

That same year, she put *The Search for Happiness* out in print with a selection of other writings. About a year later, she published another play, *The Inflexible Captive*. This was Hannah's take on an Italian opera based on a tragic story from Roman history. It appealed to popular contemporary taste for high drama and turned on classical ideas about loyalty and courage. Her friends certainly thought it was good; one wrote a prologue and Stonhouse sent a copy to his friend the actor David Garrick. Garrick was the greatest stage figure of the age and, because of this, one of the most important people in London. Not long after publication, Hannah started to make regular trips to the capital, watching Garrick perform and, in time, meeting him in person. Here was another older man who took to Hannah, encouraging her talents, helping her to meet others and seeking to protect her. It wasn't too long before *The Inflexible Captive* was performed on stage in the popular resort of Bath. Garrick's wife attended the premiere, and its success meant it travelled to Bristol too. Sally, Hannah's sister, wrote, 'All the world of Dukes,

Lords and barons were there … Never was a piece represented there known to have received so much applause!'[1] Even if we allow for a sister's natural pride, the play was a success and Hannah was definitely getting into her stride. Her new fame and friendship with the Garricks meant she now had access to London's dazzling cultural world.

The capital in the early 1770s was a thrilling place. The largest city in Europe with just over three quarters of a million inhabitants, its population was rapidly growing and would reach 1.4 million by 1815. Money from the slave trade and the East India Company's exploitation of India's resources fuelled the building of elegant squares in the West End around Oxford Street. Coffee houses were the place for men to meet and read the newly printed newspapers and magazines, whilst all kinds of people, men and women, rich and relatively poor, crowded into the two main theatres in Drury Lane and Covent Garden. Powdered hair was still normal for well-to-do men and women, whilst female outfits – for those who could afford them – were carefully constructed to produce an impressive silhouette with hair piled high adorned with feathers or bows, a tight bodice and wide skirts jutting out at the hips. In Austria, Mozart was writing operas and in France, Louis XVI and Marie Antoinette were King and Queen. Across Europe, this was an era of wit and – very often – decadence for the wealthy, though revolution was beginning to stir as ideas about the rights of men and women spread.

For much of the rest of her life she would make annual trips to the capital, but over these next few years, visits became more

1. Quoted by Mary Alden Hopkins, *Hannah More and her Circle*, (Longmans, New York; 1947), 50.

and more frequent until she became more-or-less a permanent house guest of the Garricks. The circles she joined were made up of writers, artists and thinkers. The great poet and dictionary maker, Samuel Johnson, the portraitist Sir Joshua Reynolds, as well as his painter daughter Frances, and the often outrageous gothic novelist Horace Walpole were among the many she regularly dined with. These were the kind of dinner parties which centred not on food but on witty conversation, often scribbled down afterwards, to be published later in journals. With her female friends she was part of the 'Blue Stockings', a group which gathered to discuss literature and ideas, becoming a famous 'safe space' for intellectual women. They even had their portraits painted, posing as the muses of classical mythology. Hannah posed as Melpomene, the muse representing tragedy. She looks up to the heavens, holding out a sacred cup, her brown eyes full of woe.

All this perhaps makes her seem rather serious and a bit of a social climber. Her letters tell a different story, giving a glimpse of her bubbly, busy personality. While Hannah drops plenty of names when she writes home to her sisters, and sounds part star-struck, part self-promoter, she is nearly always self-aware. Hannah mocked the society she found herself in. The 'goths and vandals, picts and saxons are come again!' she exclaims, ridiculing the fashion to powder the hair with the spice turmeric. Noble women looked 'as yellow as a crocus' when it had dripped down to stain their faces by the end of an evening.[2] When visiting rural friends who were desperate to impress, she satirises their attempts to be elegant: on their hats and hairpieces

2. Hannah More, *Letters of Hannah More*, ed. R. Brimley Johnson (Bodley Head, London: 1925), 77.

they had 'amongst them, an acre and a half of shrubbery, besides slopes, tulip beds, clumps of peonies, kitchen-gardens and green-houses'.[3] But she also laughs at herself. She mocks her surprise at winning money at cards, and even at her copious tears when Samuel Johnson read one of her poems to a room full of friends. It is as though Hannah couldn't quite believe her good fortune as a young woman of such a humble background mixing with some of the stars of the day.

While this world was opening up, Hannah's next play, *Percy*, a dramatic tale of love and revenge set in the Middle Ages, became a hit. In 1777, when she was thirty-two, the play was staged in both London theatres to rave reviews. It was so popular it was translated into French and German and put on in Europe. Mozart even owned a copy! For the next forty years, *Percy* would be part of the repertoire for many British playhouses; this is what she had dreamed of as a little girl. Had Hannah's life ended at this point or her career dwindled, she would be seen as a mildly interesting but very minor footnote in the history of female literature, with only a few plays, a handful of poems, a bundle of letters and two portraits remaining to mark her existence. But her life didn't stop at this point, and her greatest legacy is not in her literary works.[4] As is so often the case in God's strange economy, a series of disappointments led to a search for something greater than virtue or happiness, resulting in a lasting impact on society.

---

3. More, *Letters*, 9.
4. Though Hannah's works were enjoyed for a few decades after her death, later on she was viewed as a poor writer and a stuffy moralist, see for example Reginald Brimley Johnson (ed) in More, *Letters*, 1.

A new ambition

As she moved into her later-thirties, the glamour of London began to dim. First, and most significantly, David Garrick died in 1779. Her dramatic account of his state funeral in Westminster Abbey testifies compellingly to his role in her life. Having entered through the wrong door, aiming to evade the crowds, she and a friend ended up locked in a tower, only escaping through persistent shouting. She seems almost to have been numb with the shock, unsure of how to manage her life once his protection and encouragement had gone. Garrick's widow, Eva, who wasn't that much older than Hannah, encouraged her to stay on as her companion. These months of sitting about, secluded with a grieving widow became dismal, but the life of supper parties, conversation and career networking without Garrick was equally unbearable. Added to this, her next play was a flop and she faced unfounded claims of plagiarism. London life began to seem less and less appealing, and Hannah felt less and less at home. Remarkably, at least by twenty-first-century standards, she resolved that she would no longer visit the theatre.

In the Western world today, the theatre might seem a space for refined cultural expression rather than decadence; what is performed on stage so often is far tamer than what we can access on screen or even on the page. In contrast, during the eighteenth century going to plays was for many a way to be seen, to flirt and to indulge in emotional and possibly physical excess. More than this, Hannah had come to realise the complexity of her own attachment to the theatre. She loved the drama of the whole event of theatre-going, not just the play. But here was a danger. The play often encouraged her to laugh or sympathise with situations she'd otherwise see as immoral, and in seeking to write for the stage her vanity and ambition were connected to an artform she knew could cause others to stumble. Her concern for virtue, for which she was already known, was changing into something else, an awareness of her own sin. It was as if her eyes were gradually opening, not just to how much sin there was in London, but how much there was in her heart.

Playing a central part in this change was the gift of a book and the kindness of a friend. One day, Hannah's witty, intelligent friend Fanny Boscawen gave her *Cardiphonia* (meaning 'cries of the heart'). This book, small enough to fit into Hannah's pocket, was a collection of letters from John Newton, the slave trader turned vicar, to his parishioners and converts. In them, Newton warmly and clearly wrote about the Christian life:

> *The Lord in his own time returns to convince, humble, pardon, comfort and renew the soul. He touches the rock and, the waters flow ... We are gradually prepared to live more out of ourselves and to derive all our sufficiency, of every kind, from Jesus the fountain of Grace.*[5]

In pointing Hannah to the ineffectiveness of human effort and the great power and love of God, this book showed her true Christianity. Over a period of months, Hannah hid away to read. She started to listen carefully to sermons, even traipsing across London to meet Newton, and her faith shifted from a stoical sense of duty to a passionate, personal belief. Her heart's

---

5. John Newton, 'Letter to a Nobleman', *Cardiphonia*, 13-14. https://ia802608.us.archive.org/24/items/cardiphoniaorthe00newtuoft/cardiphoniaorthe00newtuoft.pdf

attention moved away from the demanding idol of reputation and towards the grace of God. She described this resolve later in print: the Christian 'will not lavish all [her] attentions on so poor a thing as [her] own advancement. [She] will desire to devote all to the only object worthy of them, to God.'[6] Hannah never regretted this choice to 'devote all' to God. She found that freedom in his love is worth any sacrifice.

6. Hannah More, *Religion of the Heart* (Paraclete Press, Mass: 1993) 38. (Originally published as Practical Piety in 1811.)

5

A New Society

Just a few years after Hannah More's heart was changed by the message of grace, a twenty-four-year-old politician, William Wilberforce, was also being affected by John Newton's ministry. Both Newton and Wilberforce had been influenced in childhood by the teaching and earnest prayers of women; Newton's mother was a non-conformist believer and Wilberforce's aunt with whom he lived for some years had been converted through the preaching of the Wesleys and George Whitefield. Both boys had turned away from these beginnings – Wilberforce briefly and fairly wildly in teenage years and early manhood, Newton for decades during which he was captain of a slave trading ship – but they turned back. Perhaps the cherished memories of these strong women of faith were what made both men come to value Hannah so highly. They both certainly knew that the belief and actions of a woman could be of great use in God's kingdom.

These great men give us a snapshot of evangelical life in Britain. Newton was twenty years younger than the Wesleys and George Whitefield and when he became a Christian minister, the revival in the UK was flourishing. Societies of converted people, men and women, up and down the country met to pray and study together, outside of church service times. Many men and some women became evangelistic preachers travelling sometimes many miles to speak to crowds in the open air. Though these groups were called 'methodists', so far there was no denomination of this name. The movement's leaders were ordained Church of England ministers. They had good relationships with many independent churches, uniting around the central truths of the gospel and the need for a heart response to Christ. There was opposition, though, from many Church of England leaders, who saw the revival as dangerous and disruptive 'enthusiasm'. This disdain was there in society at large, too. Wilberforce, when he met with Newton early on, reminded him, 'remember that I must be secret'.[1] Preachers were sometimes attacked in the streets and mocked in the newspapers. Then, as now, evangelicals were suspect.

John Newton at different times had to urge both Wilberforce and Hannah not to retreat from public life. It was tempting to withdraw from the world in which they had been living, knowing that they might well be laughed at, and now seeing clearly the ugliness of sin and corruption around them. Wilberforce had to be persuaded to stay in politics, and Hannah was encouraged to use her gifts of writing and sociability for good. Despite the network they were both part of, it was only in 1787, two years after Wilberforce first took communion indicating his assurance

1. Quoted by Marylynn Rouse, 'A Double Portion of My thoughts and Prayers', The John Newton Project, 2002, https://www.johnnewton.org/Articles/105307/The_John_Newton/archive/The_Complete_Works/Correspondence/William_Wilberforce/background.aspx

of faith, that the two met in the elegant surroundings of Bath and immediately hit it off. They were both alike in so many ways, having a great talent for friendship and a quick wittedness which made them impressive communicators in both speech and writing. What's more, they both had a huge sense of humour. It is no wonder that they stayed in touch until their dying days. Not long after this memorable meeting, they together became involved in a campaign which would dominate the remainder of their lives.

The great battle begins

Thousands of miles away from the theatres of London and the Spa at Bath – but funding so much of the luxury in those places – was the exploitation of thousands and thousands of African people. Rebecca Protten may have been set free decades before but the evil continued, and even grew. At the same time, revulsion against the slave trade was also growing. Years before they came to faith, both Hannah and William had taken a stand against slavery. Searching for a topic for a school essay, fourteen-year-old William had chosen to write about how wrong the trade was, and Hannah in her twenties had been ready to argue with several friends about it. Christian tradition was clearly against slavery, as Quakers pointed out citing the history and writers of the early church. Enlightenment philosophy, too, with its emphasis on the rights of the individual and interest in the value of feelings, made the idea that one person could be owned by another seem outrageous. Added to this, as the trade in flesh had grown, truths where exposed about the brutality of the middle passage, where kidnapped Africans such as Rebecca's mother were crammed into overcrowded ships.

The notorious case of the Zong in 1783, horrified the nation. The captain of the heavily-loaded slave ship claimed that it was running low on water and so 130 of the hundreds of captives it carried were thrown overboard to preserve the remainder. What made this massacre even more shocking was that it came to court as an insurance claim; people were being treated as disposable assets, their bodies seen as ballast to be dumped when required. Around this time, books were being printed to expose the day-to-day oppression of people by planters in the Caribbean, and these stories were backed up by the testimonies of emancipated individuals like Olaudah Equiano, born the same year as Hannah, who had made a home in England. On the streets of Bristol you could occasionally meet slaves working for white families and in the harbour, you could find ships, minus their human cargo, ready to sail; the reminders of this deathly trade were hard to avoid. Yet, the wealth it generated was enriching many people and fuelling exciting new industries. The flourishing elegance and the impressive technological advances of the eighteenth century were invisibly tied to it. Slavery seemed an immovable fact of life; you could argue against it, but to imagine it ending was to deal in fantasy.

Something remarkable, however, began to happen in the second half of the 1780s. An extraordinary network of individuals came together, united by their dream of ending slavery. Some were Quakers, who had been staunchly anti-slavery for decades, and many others were evangelical believers. They dared to move from philosophical argument to political strategy, so that a dream could become reality. In 1787, the committee for the Abolition for the Slave Trade was founded with key members Granville Sharpe and Thomas Clarkson, both evangelicals who had begun to work together doing research and campaigning. One of their group, Hannah's friend Margaret Middleton, approached William Wilberforce, asking if he would be the parliamentary face for the campaign. Wilberforce's agreement was a great coup. The movement was gaining momentum, and quickly many more were brought on board.

Barham Court in the pretty village of Teston in Kent, might seem an unlikely headquarters for this activist movement. The house still stands today, looking like a grand wedding cake: a vast white stucco façade, evenly adorned with pediments and large windows. This was the home of the Middletons. She was a painter, on the edges of Hannah's refined London set of friends, and he had risen through the ranks to become one of the most senior Naval commanders in the country. By the 1880s, he had a seat in Parliament and was awarded a knighthood. Having achieved such social privilege, he could have been tempted to sit back and enjoy it. The experience of Sir Middleton and his friend, the local vicar, once his ship's surgeon, meant that this couldn't happen. Years before, they had intercepted a slave ship at sea. On board they found slaves crammed together in the lower decks, the floors wet with blood and excrement. This vivid memory set the course for both men. They began writing and speaking for the cause, welcoming many others including Hannah to their large home to talk, plan and pray about what could be done.

Hannah decided, unsurprisingly, to write. Her poem *Slavery* was published in 1788 and dramatises in her usual rhyming couplets not only the cruel treatment of Africans, but also the gross attitudes which underlay it. She emphasises the equality of all people, despite outward differences, and reasons that racism, before that word had been coined, was behind the trade, asking, 'What strange offence, what aggravated sin? They stand convicted – of a darker skin!'[2] The traders, Hannah claims, are the 'barbarians'; the white man is the 'savage', not the African. The poem that starts with Enlightenment reasoning ends with Christian preaching. The slave trade will make Africans despise the Christian God who died for them, but, she prophesies, God is working to bring his light and freedom to Africa. The trade will end and God's kingdom will come. This poem was a partner to the research and testimonies of the male campaigners. It was relatively short (you can read it in about an hour), cheap to buy and as a poem, could be very accessible to polite women who might not pick up more 'political works'. The poem was a success and paved the way for more activism of another polite kind.

Women could not vote in eighteenth century Britain – that right was well over a hundred years away – but they did have other forms of political power. The speeches in parliament were only really effective because of evidence that public opinion was changing. Local groups through the country, often dominated by women, quickly organised petitions which were brought to parliament: in Manchester this was so successful that over twenty per cent of the population signed. Even more powerful, perhaps, was the female-led boycott of West Indian sugar which was grown exclusively through the labours of enslaved people. Hannah More was one of the first to become an 'anti-saccharite' and kept this up throughout her life. In the 1890s, at the height of the boycott, it is said that the national demand for sugar dropped significantly, challenging the profits of plantation owners.

2. Hannah More, *Slavery: A Poem* (T Caddell, London: 1788), 8.

Hannah never let the campaign against the slave trade drop. She spoke to her powerful friends and she supported the politicians and church leaders who made a public stand against slavery through her warm and frequent letters. She also continued to publish poems and short stories which argued emotively for abolition through the next few decades, keeping up the pressure as the fight went on and on. For although public opinion was supportive of change, the vested interests of wealthy politicians and the establishment's fear of social upheaval, stirred by the French Revolution of 1797, meant that British trading in humans wasn't outlawed until 1807. The law forbidding ownership of people as slaves took another twenty-six years. It was passed in July 1833, when Wilberforce was on his deathbed. Hannah More herself died just one month later. It had been a long and tumultuous battle. A times, Hannah and her friends may have wondered whether their efforts were ever going to make a difference, but in God's strength and with God's compassion they persevered. We can praise God for them and pray that he will raise up Christians today to carry on the long fight against the many injustices which still abound.

Changing lives at home

Abolition was important to Hannah, but it wasn't her only concern. She and her Christian friends were very troubled by the careless lives of the privileged people they knew. It was right to fight against evils committed far away but they knew they couldn't be silent about the less obvious but still destructive sins they could see all around. In the early 1780s, Wilberforce discovered how many prisoners were being tried and executed in Britain. He was horrified by the numbers of people dying for their crimes. The death penalty was routinely applied for cases of theft, assault and murder, for men and women of all ages. He was also keenly aware, after his years studying at Cambridge, of the corrupt behaviour of the fashionable wealthy. Gambling, heavy drinking and wastefulness were routine among the gentry. As the Industrial Revolution took off through the country, the middle classes were flourishing too. They indulged their taste for showing off new houses and glamorous interiors and spent their days getting noticed at card games and dinners. For the newly converted Wilberforce, this data painted a picture of a careless nation in which all classes were hardened to God and his standards. The nation, he feared, was ripe for God's judgement.

Wilberforce learned also of societies which had been set up in previous generations, often by religious people, for the 'reformation of manners'. These groups had existed, in the absence of anything like our modern form of policing, to clamp down on anti-social activity like sabbath breaking, prostitution, public swearing and other forms of disorder, issuing fines and sometimes imprisonment. This discovery led Wilberforce, and in turn Hannah More, to act. He famously declared in 1787, 'God Almighty has set before me two great objects, the suppression of the slave trade and the reformation of manners.'[3] For them both, political change had to be accompanied by personal, local change. But, despite language similar to earlier attempts, this new campaign didn't seek to 'reform manners' through hounding the poor in legal prosecutions. Instead, using persuasion and gospel

---

3. Quoted by William E. Phipps, *Amazing Grace in John Newton: Slave Ship Captain, Hymn Writer, and Abolitionist* (Mercere University Press, Georgia: 2001), 182.

proclamation, this time the behaviour of the well-to-do would be challenged.

In that same year, Hannah More wrote a book to do precisely this, supporting Wilberforce in his attempts. Her title *Thoughts on the Importance of the Manners of the Great* seems perhaps a little flattering to her audience, but there is plenty that is hard hitting between the covers. How different this work is from her 1777 selection of *Essays on Various Subjects*, a so-called 'conduct book', which preaches the importance of right behaviour for young women. Having come to mature faith in Christ, she now pulls no punches. The reality of God's judgement is clearly presented and the socially 'great' are shown to be in danger; she pointedly describes Herod and Ananias and Sapphira, amongst others, as examples of people who were complacent, caring about outward respectability, but inwardly cool towards God. Christianity is a religion of the heart, she insists, and God's standard is one of perfection.

Despite this challenge, Hannah is coy. She says that she isn't 'an old man, a clergyman or a methodist', so this isn't a sermon.[4] Hannah doesn't dwell on doctrine or what the 'faith', which she says is central, consists of. Instead her concentration is on heart obedience. She skewers the women who will give generously to foreign missions but employ hairdressers on a Sunday, therefore preventing them from hearing the gospel at church, and mocks the heads of household who will pay for the instruction of others but won't lead family devotions in their own homes. She interrogates leisure pursuits: are concerts and pleasure

4. Hannah More, *Thoughts on the Manners of the Great* (T Caddell, London: 1788), 21.

gardens really good if they make us forget the gospel? Modern readers might find her emphasis on a very strict sabbath and her negativity about aspects of culture off-putting but reading closely, we can see that her heart is for the common people and for Christ. Hannah wants all people to see how good God is, and she hates the thought that the carelessness of the wealthy will prevent the poor from accessing this truth. Nominal Christianity, she argues, is worse than nothing.

Hannah followed up this book with another similar book six years later in which she again targets the self-interested rich, calling them with even more passion to a whole-hearted love for God.[5] A few more years and Wilberforce would write a similar book with the very convoluted title, *A Practical View of the Prevailing Religious System of Professed Christians, in the Higher and Middle Classes in this Country, Compared with Real Christianity*. His work was perhaps yet more explicit about the gospel, but both of them were wanting and working for the same thing: a society transformed by real trust in Christ. As one historian writes, they 'set out to make religion fashionable'.[6]

Their conviction that the good of all is best served by seeking to influence those at the top of the social tree has been a key thread in British evangelicalism up to the present day. By prioritising leaders of politics and law, as well as land-owners, employers and even the Royal Family (Hannah wrote a whole book full of advice to the heir to the throne, Princess Charlotte),

---

5. Hannah More, *Estimate of the Religion of the Fashionable World*. By One of the Laity (1793).
6. Jonathan Bayes, *William Wilberforce: His Impact on Nineteenth-Century Society Churchman*, 108/2, 1994, https://bit.ly/3fXkBWr

these evangelicals might seem to have been snobbish, paying excessive attention to those at the top of the pile. There is some truth in that accusation. Hannah More and her friends were instinctively conservative and they had no desire to disrupt the rigid class system of the day. Yet, their chosen focus did mean that the lives of many were changed for good. The development of a serious Christian culture among the privileged led to laws protecting factory workers, prison reform and support for struggling women. There's an anecdote that a member of the aristocracy stopped getting her hair done on a Sunday because of Hannah's arguments. Maybe that seems a laughably small impact after so many earnest words, but if it meant that by it two women, one of great wealth, another of relative poverty, were freed to worship, then Hannah would definitely have seen it as a success. Out of small steps, movements grow.

A new community

The fact that Hannah was an active collaborator with a group of public men didn't go unnoticed by others. Radical MP William Cobbet snidely called her a 'Prelate [bishop] in petticoats'.[7] He thought that she was interfering in affairs not her own, with an authority which was unfitting. The circle of Wilberforce's friends, who were later called 'The Clapham Sect' after the area where many of them lived, didn't seem to think so. Current historians include her as a key contributor alongside Granville Sharp, Thomas Clarkson, wealthy banker John Thornton, local vicar John Venn, one-time plantation overseer Zachary

---

7. William Cobbett, 'To Mr Brougham', in *Cobbett's Political Register Volume 69* (Cobbett, London: 1830), 711.

Macaulay and the prominent lawyer James Stephen. Together they were involved in schemes like establishing Sierra Leone as a home for emancipated slaves and campaigning for missionaries to be allowed into India, as well as the foundation of the Church Missionary Society and the British and Foreign Bible Society. They sought to challenge the use of young boys as chimney sweeps, argued for welfare reform and better provision of hospitals. The world of Clapham was filled with action, ideas and responsibility.

Most of these men were married to intelligent, educated wives, but these women resisted taking a public role. They educated their children, provided hospitality and supported their husbands – no small task when many were embroiled in significant political battles and their families were large. Wilberforce wrote tellingly in his *Practical View* of his belief that women were more prone to religious feeling than men, and so wives had a special and high calling to put their faith to use in training children and stirring up the hearts of their husbands. Pressure was on for Clapham wives to prove to the world his ideas. Hannah More, as a single woman, was excused this elevated though restricted role. She could enjoy being a doting godmother to some of the many Clapham children. They loved eating strawberries on her lawn and treasured the books she gave them. The pets she kept and her lovely gardens must have made visits such fun. But then they would go home and Hannah could get on with writing, strategising and advising their fathers. She didn't have the delights of parenthood and the intimacy of marriage, but neither the dangers of childbirth and the dreadful loss of children which so many suffered. Supported by her four sisters, with whom she lived for much of the rest of her life, she could move about the country, start her own schemes, make her own charitable donations, purchase property and maintain friendships with a range of prominent men and their wives.

6

Back to Schools

Not long after giving up the theatre, Hannah moved back to the South-west of England and into a house not too far from the village where she had been born. Her sisters by this point had given up their school and moved to Bath, and her parents had died. Cowslip Green was the suitably picturesque name of the cottage which would become a base for her and Patty, her closest sister. Much of the winter would still be spent in London with Eva, Garrick's widow, escaping the damp and cold. There would also be trips to Bath and Teston, but Cowslip Green offered freedom and independence, a place where she was mistress. Properly now she had a home of her own, not a borrowed or rented room, where she could write and be hostess to a procession of visitors. Tucked away down a lane outside the village of Wrington, the house itself was quite small but it had a large garden. Writing to John Newton, she asked if gardening was a good hobby for a Christian; she feared that it was just too distracting for her heart. Having come to know Christ in the middle of her life, she now didn't want to waste any of it in unworthy pursuits. But Hannah loved the creativity of choosing plants and planting her flower beds. It was such a pleasure to be outside, hearing the birds and getting her hands dirty pruning and weeding, then watching the buds grow and bloom. What a relief to her tender conscience when Newton, surely smiling to himself, gave her the go-ahead. Hannah could certainly testify to the importance of seeking the counsel of wise friends!

With such a right concern for making the most of her time, it was probably inevitable that when William Wilberforce visited Hannah in 1789 and made a suggestion about another project, she took him very seriously. His journey around the wider area during his stay had been distressing. He'd seen tremendous poverty and, having stopped to talk to locals, had discovered how deep the problems were. In the Cheddar Gorge, where the famous cheese was and still is manufactured, many families lived in caves, their children in rags. The romantic scenery was wild with steep outcrops of limestone rock, jutting out of the lush Somerset hills, but life here was far from a rustic dream. Most families lived in thrall to a few, often hard-headed, farmers, earning a precarious income from hard manual work. Like most villages, there was no school and worse, though not uncommon, there was no resident vicar to oversee charitable support or provide pastoral care and Bible teaching. Wilberforce, Hannah and Patty together agreed that 'something must be done'.[1]

That something would become a project which would dominate the remainder of Hannah More's life. It would harness

1. Quoted by Martha More, Mendip Annals: Or a Narrative of the Charitable Labours of Hannah and Martha More in their Neighbourhood: Being the Journal of Martha More (New York, Carter and Brothers: 1859), 47.

many of the skills she'd already employed in campaigning, teaching and writing but would bring her a level of opposition she'd never encountered before. Patty would be her chief ally in this work, taking a significant share in establishing at first one school in the village of Cheddar and, over the space of a few years, nine others in surrounding villages. Wilberforce was the primary benefactor, offering to cover the costs of their first enterprise, but Hannah quickly found out that money wasn't the main problem at all.

Tackling the wealthy

Visiting Cheddar, Hannah discovered that all Wilberforce had said was true, but what was at least as troubling as the ignorance and poverty of the villagers was the disinterest of their employers. Starting right away, she travelled from farm to farm on a charm offensive. Oh the 'petty tyrants whose insolence I stroked and tamed, ugly children I fondled, the pointers and spaniels I caressed, the cyder I commended, the wine I drank'![2] What she encountered was a fear of education and religion; like plantation owners in the Caribbean, these employers, hardly educated themselves, thought that both would make the poor harder to control. Hannah's persuasion tactic was to claim that a school would produce law abiding workers and would occupy them on a Sunday, keeping them out of mischief. In this argument she was walking a tightrope, which she herself probably didn't fully understand. She didn't have any real desire to upset the social system and in fact was, especially later in life, resistant to the idea that the poor masses should have access to a literary education,

2. More, *Letters*, 164.

believing the basics of reading and craft skills good enough for those who would always be of the servant class. At the same time, she went on to employ working class teachers in her schools and poured out her own money to supply needs with great compassion and care. Like so many of us, Hannah wasn't always consistent! Ultimately, it was God's glory and salvation for souls which motivated her, not any political vision either of hierarchy or equality.

Hannah's pattern and aims were the same in most places even though the villages, though so close together, were quite different in make-up. Cheddar was agricultural, and poverty was great. Other places were dominated by the mining or the glass-making industry. In some of these villages there might be less poverty, but money earned was spent quickly on drink and the lives of workers were often chaotic. Underground working conditions with furnaces were terrifying and catastrophic accidents could happen at any time with no insurance or welfare support to cover loss. In one village a woman was sentenced to death for her part in a riot over the price of butter; in other places unscrupulous bakers consistently used inaccurate weights for bread, a staple on which the poor relied. It was a world away from the genteel social whirl of London from which Hannah had retreated, but the difference didn't appear to daunt her, instead it galvanised her desire to act.

Together with Patty, Hannah set schools in place in these few villages, which were open on Sundays to teach children over the age of six to read and memorise simple Bible truths. They sent away noisy toddlers and, realising that their good work could be undone so quickly in homes with illiterate parents, invited adults to come to evening classes. In Cheddar they employed an older woman and her daughter to teach, paying them well. These two added pastoral visits in the village to their duties. Hannah said that they did what any conscientious vicar would have done, praying with the sick and offering words of comfort, as well as often organising practical help, including money and medicine. Hannah and Patty were in no way trying to replace the established church authorities, but they were showing that there was too much spiritual need around for ministry to be limited to ordained men. They knew that women could bring the comfort of faith to people, men and women, young and old.

This ministry of the good news had very practical outworkings. When they came to understand that young people often didn't attend church because their clothes were in such a poor state, the More sisters started to give donations of shoes, stockings and caps to their pupils. They began supporting clubs for the women, a system that normally operated for employed men. By paying a penny and a half a week into the club fund, women could then receive a kind of maternity or sick pay if and when needed, or even a donation to cover funeral costs. They employed people to teach practical skills to the children, such as knitting and spinning or household skills, so girls could find employment once they were grown. But Hannah and Patty's action wasn't just aimed at treating the symptoms of injustice. They wrote to their Clapham MP friends requesting that these issues be raised in Parliament, and where local gentry were squeezing the poor, they faced up to them, demanding that those who had power had an obligation to care for the needy. The Mores' social conservatism had no patience with either selfish capitalism or aristocratic callousness.

The heart of the work, however, was always gospel-focused. Books were made prizes for learning the catechism; prayers or Scripture verses were handed out regularly along with gingerbread as a treat for good behaviour. Once a year, a great feast was held with a procession out of the village on to a hillside where there would be songs, a sermon and a lavish picnic of roast beef, plum pudding and cake. New teachers were identified from amongst the local working people; one had been a milkmaid and another a farm labourer. These were then trained and paid by the Mores, who aimed to visit two of the schools each Sunday, walking or riding their horses through the rough country lanes to do so, whatever the weather. Hannah and Patty rolled up their sleeves to support their paid teachers. They taught the children, telling Bible stories with great energy and helping the children remember the back-and-forth questions and answers of the catechism. What might seem dry to a twenty-first-century child, was gripping for those without books or screens. To learn that they were made for a purpose – to know the Creator of the world – and that they were loved with a fierce, undying care was simply life changing for those whose lives were fragile and hard. For the sisters the work was relentless, but thrilling. What a privilege it was, and is, to work alongside God to bring this bright hope to others!

Weary but rejoicing

Hannah More wasn't the first to set up Sunday Schools for the poor. There are a few examples from as early as the 1600s, but the movement is recognised as having started in earnest just a few years prior to the Cheddar school by Robert Raikes in Gloucester. Raikes started a school in a kitchen for the poor children of his district and inspired many others to follow suit, beginning a national surge in provision of schooling for the very poor. Sarah Trimmer was another notable Sunday School leader whom Hannah More got to know. She not only taught her twelve children and set up a school but wrote delightful, ground-breaking reading primers and books on the principles of education. What Hannah accomplished, however, went beyond these other examples. She and Patty ran a network of schools. By 1796, the pupils being taught across the villages numbered over 1,500 and in many of the villages, after a school was established, several other enterprises reaching into the wider community followed.

The More schools became an institution central to village life and through them lives changed for the better. Many came to a lively Christian faith; in Cheddar the church congregation grew by over 1,000 per cent. With her connections she was able to get good Bible teachers appointed to be curates in some of the villages. Apprentices who had been spending their scant wages and leisure time on gambling or drink, now enjoyed serious conversation and reading. Many others found their lives changed by practical help the sisters offered. In some villages, Hannah organised the building of a communal oven to save the cost of fuel and the burden of work for the poorest families. She even supplied thrifty recipes and bought rice in bulk so that good food could be prepared more cheaply. Some might argue this merging of practical aid and spiritual outreach is an attempt to manipulate the poor. It could look as though Hannah was imposing middle-class values on the local working-class culture, moulding people to fit her own sensibilities. Perhaps she was. But she saw first-hand the misery of life, especially for women and children, in places where poverty and hard drinking went hand in hand, and tried her best to help those whom no one else was helping.

It was not long before some decided the More schools were a threat to the power of the church and ruling authorities. Across the English Channel events were unfolding which explain some of the opposition she was to face. In the same year Hannah was persuading farmers to give their servants permission to learn, the infamous Bastille Prison in Paris was stormed and the French Revolution began. To begin with, Hannah celebrated. The monarchy was obviously corrupt and so the introduction of democracy could only be a good thing; wasn't this an opportunity for freedom of religion and an end to oppression? Quickly, it became clear that this wasn't the case, as aristocrats began to be executed and civil war broke out. In 'The Terror' of 1793-94, it is estimated that 17,000 people were guillotined and a further 10,000 died in prison, including many Catholic priests.

It is no wonder that in the ten years Hannah was establishing schools she met with furious opposition even after she had won round the village authorities. Authorities of all kinds feared that to give oppressed and uneducated people instant political liberty could bring disaster for the whole country. This was mixed, in the opposition to Hannah, with misogyny and also, specifically, a dislike of the religious focus of the schools. By this time, Wesley's groups had broken from the Anglican church to become their own denomination and the fear of 'enthusiasm' had subsequently increased; no longer was there just a suspicion that religious seriousness involved irrational, emotional religious behaviour, but also real prejudice from some establishment figures at anything which seemed not to conform to the Church of England's practices. These fears and prejudices resulted in broken windows and a long legal and publishing campaign which would lead Hannah to a physical breakdown.

Today we're used to social media trolling and online slander. These tend to be fast and furious – horrible for those living through them, but very often blowing over after a number of months. For Hannah More the persecution lasted years. It focused on accusations that a teacher of hers was holding Methodist gatherings, in which he prayed his own prayers rather than using the Anglican prayer book. In the period of revolution, this deviation from sanctioned liturgy spoke of lawlessness. It was blown up further still in the pamphlets that were distributed in London and posters which were pasted to trees and walls in the village. The More sisters were dangerous radicals, disloyal to the nation, untrustworthy and even unbelievers. Although at a legal hearing Hannah agreed to close the school, the smear campaign went on. Ironically, it was led by the vicar of the parish who had started to argue against the teaching of the Apostle Paul and belief in the Trinity. Hannah published her own pamphlets in defence of her work, but didn't attack her attackers and eventually, three years after it started, the voices died down and faded away. Hannah retreated to her bed for months, suffering from headaches and asthma, emotionally overwhelmed by all she'd endured. Hannah had tried to walk a tightrope and suffered for it.

The truth is that Hannah did employ Methodists and she counted Methodists among her friends, though she had qualms about some of their activities. She also had high church (Anglican traditionalist) supporters, though again, she didn't agree with them totally. Hannah had a large heart and she wanted to work with others who loved the gospel, not just those of a similar background or denominational identity. No doubt, though, she and her sisters found themselves under greater scrutiny than men in similar situations would have been. They were unmarried women who at times challenged male leaders and acted on their own initiative. They did this with great tact and respect, but their higher loyalty to the urgent demand of gospel proclamation, meant that they didn't give up easily, or fit into a neat box. Despite their readiness to submit to Scripture, to some looking on, these middle-aged sisters really did seem a threat to the status quo.

Hannah's exhaustion was deep, but through it all, the faithful sisters maintained the schools, and the work went on. Despite her ill health and increasing age, Hannah was able to write from her bed. There was always a letter to be dashed off – a light hearted one to her old London friends or a report for her financial backers – and frequently there was a book to start or edit. The list of Hannah's publications is long and diverse; to her plays and books of advice, she added popular short stories and ballads in the 1970s. Having taught working-class people to read, she now had to provide something for them to enjoy. There were 'chap books' cheaply available already, rather like the gossip magazines, tabloid newspapers or 'airport novels' of today. These had stories of scandal and romance. There were also political pamphlets catering for the newly literate as well as sometimes offering extremist manifestos. Hannah felt that none of this was safe for those she had laboured to teach and disciple. The Christian beliefs and values of loyalty and hard work could easily be lost through these secular romances or what she saw as dangerous politically, radical literature.

In 1792, her friend the Bishop of London had begged her to write something to address the radical ideas spreading around the country through books like *The Rights of Man* by Thomas Paine. Hannah obliged with first one, then three more tracts which, through dialogue and simple story, try to persuade the reader that the ideas of the French Revolution are bad news and that hard work is the best way to reform. Unsurprisingly, Hannah worked with others to supply this need. Roping in financial backers and other writers she created a set of easy to read, highly moralistic stories. These preach contentment for the poor and the dangers of sin. The good are happy and the wicked end up punished. None can be considered great literature, but the details of working life in them show that she knew the country and the way people lived in the villages around her.

A little girl, whose first memories were of books and stories, ended her life writing, reading and talking about books. One by one, over a period of twenty years, her dear sisters died, leaving her alone in her cottage with its cherished garden, her pets, a couple of servants and plenty of visitors. She was a well-known old lady and politicians and writers still came to listen to her, among them William Gladstone, who would become prime minister, the poet William Wordsworth, and her godson, the brilliant historian Thomas Macaulay. She had lived in a different age from the new Victorian era which was dawning; many of the campaigns she had fought had been won and the changes she had longed for had been realised. Evangelicalism had become a powerful force, missionaries were preaching in many new areas, Christian education and care for the poor was flourishing and, a few weeks before her death in 1833, the possession of slaves on British territory was outlawed. Though many would go on to criticise the real limitations in her view of the poor and the quality of her writing, she had succeeded in changing lives for the better.

Eventually she became so weak and vulnerable that she wasn't able to manage her household. Servants she had trusted were abusing their privileges and exploiting their boss, partying in her home while she was confined to bed upstairs. It was a sad end to so many years trying to help the working classes. Hannah wasn't bitter. She lived a very long life and now was weak and tired. She moved into the city and it was there that she died on 7 September 1833 aged eighty-eight. Her strength had been spent in great labours which would live on after her; Hannah's schools remained and her books were read by a new generation. The wealth she had given away was being used all over the globe to bring others to know Christ. At the end, she knew the truth of the words she herself had written in her book on holiness years before:

> *There is an inward peace in a humble trust in God and a simple reliance on His Word. There is a repose of spirit, a freedom from worry in the lowly confidence in Him, for which the world has nothing to give in exchange.*[3]

3. More, *Religion of the Heart*, 56.

London's Tireless Labourer

ELLEN RANYARD,

1810-1879

7

The Challenging Teen

Ellen White (later Ranyard) was born in 1810. The England she entered was very different from the one Hannah was born into just sixty-five years before. God had used Moravians like Rebecca Protten, who had died thirty years previously, to play their part in the evangelical revival, which led to the work of the Clapham Sect pressing for transformation in society. There were campaigns afoot to limit factory hours to protect children and to prevent cruelty to animals. More and more schools were being established to provide for the poor and for girls. This was a time of increasingly rapid industrial development, technical advances and new discoveries overseas; it was the period of Jane Austen's and Mary Shelley's novels and the poetry of Wordsworth, Coleridge and Shelley. It perhaps seemed as if Britain was flourishing in this late Georgian heyday.

That is one way of viewing these few decades. We could, though, also look at the great poverty in the country as industrialisation raced ahead and many flocked to the cities to work in the new factories where there was little protection for employees. Britain was still a far from democratic place, with less than three per cent of the population having the vote, and real limitations on who could enter the professions or attend university. Brilliant women, like Hannah More and others, may have been publishing books and contributing to reform, and wealthy women too could play a role behind the scenes as patrons or influencers, but mostly, like working class men, their opportunities were limited. Born into a middle-class family in London, Ellen Ranyard certainly had few public expectations placed on her. Instead it seems that she was educated for life as a wife and mother. We know little of her early life, because the details Ellen left behind are sketchy. She really didn't want people to be focused on her.

Nine Elms, where Ellen grew up, is now gleaming with office developments and prestigious blocks of flats. In the year of her birth, however, this area on the south bank of the Thames was filled with market gardens supplying the expanding city and industry. Ellen's father had built a profitable cement works here, and from the windows of the White's home the brick chimneys of his bottle shaped kilns could be seen pumping out plumes of white smoke six days a week. Steam engines were used to convert the raw materials of clay and lime into cement. This wasn't a clean or elegant business, but it was important. New technologies allowed men like Ellen Ranyard's father to make essential goods more quickly and effectively than ever before, fuelling the industrial and financial boom years of Britain.

Ellen grew up in a household where hard work was prized and an entrepreneurial spirit celebrated. She and her five younger siblings had all that they needed. There was no anxiety about earning a living for Ellen, unlike for Hannah More and her sisters. Ellen's parents had moved up in the world, arriving in the wealthy middle classes and so her education was to equip her to slot comfortably into this new world. The Whites could afford to keep Ellen and her sister at home as they grew into adulthood, playing the part of domesticated and pleasant young ladies, while her brothers carried on the business and joined the professions.

Middle class status and security wasn't the family's main concern, however. Ellen's mother and father had both been baptised as infants in Anglican parishes, but somewhere along the way they had joined an independent evangelical church. They were living the serious life which Hannah More and William Wilberforce had urged people to consider a decade or so before. The reformation of manners was taking place bit by bit as families like Ellen's shaped their lives around the gospel. In their comfortable home, the family and their few servants gathered for worship every day as Ellen's father, John White, read a passage of the Bible and prayed. The children learnt Bible passages and the answers to the shorter catechism. Ellen told others that her father was a gentle man, so the times when he sat down with her to explain God's Word on a Sunday afternoon, resting from his long working week, were sweet and precious.

Ellen's mother was in contrast a stern woman. Responsible for her children's education, she was a sharp disciplinarian. Time was God's good gift and it had to be used well. Something of this early training stayed with Ellen throughout adulthood, along with the enjoyment of the more refined things in life. The family may have been serious Christians, but this didn't prevent them, nor others like them, from embracing books, art and in-depth study. Ellen learned to draw and paint and was encouraged to read widely. As she grew into her teens she loved Byron's romantic poetry and reading the *Literary Review*. But even as she enjoyed her easy life, one doubt nagged at her. She was not sure she was saved.

The greatest change

In 1826, when Ellen was sixteen, things changed. She wrote later in life of how her parents took her to a Bible meeting in Wanstead, then a village outside of London. The thirteen-mile journey was too far for a day trip and so the White family stayed over with another family, and it was there that Ellen met Elizabeth Saunders. Elizabeth was a similar age and a lonely girl. Her only Christian friend, through whom she had been converted, had just moved out of the area. Though her parents didn't condemn her faith, they didn't encourage it either. Elizabeth felt isolated, and what's more, she struggled with her health. Ellen felt sorry for her, and so did her mother. Together they made a plan for Elizabeth to travel back to Nine Elms with them for a break.

It was supposed to be a rest, but Elizabeth was a passionate girl and her concern for those who didn't know Christ troubled her. She probed Ellen, asking, 'Have you ever thought what you will do with your life?' Ellen was rather taken aback and replied that she would, 'Go on cultivating my mind and my faculties',[1] an answer which didn't satisfy her friend. Like so many women of her class, Ellen was pursuing education for no ultimate end other than self-enhancement. There seemed no other real way

1. Quoted by Lizzie Alldridge, *The World's Workers: Florence Nightingale, Frances Ridley Havergal, Catherine Marsh, Mrs Ranyard*, (Cassell and Company, London: 1885), 105.

of using her studies. But Elizabeth, like Hannah More, saw the possibility of a greater purpose. She argued, 'This cultivation is to enable you the better to live for others, not for yourself',[2] and kept on at Ellen: Didn't she love the Bible? Didn't she care that others didn't have a copy for themselves? Reluctantly, Ellen admitted that she hadn't really given these things much thought, despite her parents' seriousness about faith. So they set out together into the streets around Nine Elms, two sixteen-year-olds armed with a Bible and a notebook. Ellen recounts how the notebook had been neatly marked with a grid in preparation for their walk. Elizabeth knew what she was doing – this was no idle saunter but a serious task, planned and prepared in advance.

The British and Foreign Bible Society had been set up in 1804, just a few years before Ellen's birth, by Wilberforce and friends. Unlike other, earlier societies, it was deliberately non-denominational. It aimed to get Bibles into the hands of as many people and as many places as possible. In this way it was a typical result of the Evangelical Revival, uniting Christians around a belief in the need for personal salvation, the centrality of Scripture and the importance of Christ's work on the cross. From the start it was a flexible organisation, making the most of women's energies and local groups to both raise money and distribute Bibles. And this was in large part because of the female inspiration for the organisation. Mary Jones was a poor girl, the daughter of a weaver in remote mid-Wales. Many Christian children, even today, have grown up hearing her story of how she saved pennies for six years to buy a Welsh language Bible for herself and her family, and then how, finally, at the age of fifteen,

2. Alldridge, *The World's Workers*, 105.

she trekked 26 miles to the nearest town to buy a Bible from the minister, Thomas Charles. This godly minister was so moved by Mary's persistence, and the scarcity of the Bibles in Wales, that he proposed to the Religious Tract Society (the organisation founded to supply tracts, many written by Hannah More) that a new Society should be formed. With the story of a brave and determined young woman at the centre of the movement, it was unsurprising that women became its prime supporters.

Elizabeth, despite her age, lack of parental support and physical weakness, was already involved in a local branch of the Bible Society as a 'Bible Collector'. She may have been directly inspired by Mary Jones perhaps; she was certainly passionate about her role. Ellen's mother insisted that she drink a rather disgusting sounding egg and wine concoction before she left the house to strengthen her as she set out with a dual mission: to wake up Ellen from her spiritual complacency and to offer cheap Bibles to those they met. They spoke to people in the street and knocked on doors. Those who didn't have Bibles were offered the opportunity to buy one at reduced rates, paying a penny (roughly the equivalent of fifty pence today) a week for a number of months. Those who did have Bibles were asked if they wanted to make a donation to provide for others. It was a simple scheme and on that day, amazingly, the two girls managed to sign up thirty-five householders. Thirty-five pennies went in their collecting bag and thirty-five addresses in their book.

On their route, Elizabeth and Ellen had stepped into a run-down shop where an old woman was selling coal and some vegetables. The strange mixture made for a horrible smell and the woman was especially rude to the girls. Late in life, Ellen still remembered this shocking moment of seeing how others lived – just a short walk from her home – in circumstances so very different from her 'cultivated' drawing room world. Ellen may have been used to hearing about mission and even praying for it dutifully with her family, but the reality was a shock.

What also stuck in her mind, and in fact, completely transformed her life, were the events of the next few days. Ellen went to bed that night and picked up her own Bible. She had been drilled to read a chapter a night since she was first able to read, but this time it was different. She opened up Genesis 1, and as she read 'Let there be light', the words affected her in a new way. Ellen wrote that 'there was light upon its pages never seen before' and she felt 'a quiet new affection'.[3] Elizabeth's passion for Christ stirred up a new love in Ellen, giving her a gentleness and peace which she would need over the next few weeks.

Elizabeth and Ellen were both tired and ill after their Bible collecting round. Ellen recovered after a day, but Elizabeth didn't. Symptoms of typhoid appeared: a high fever, cough, listlessness and loss of appetite. This disease, treatable now, was fatal in 1826. Elizabeth was too ill to be returned to her own home so in Nine Elms, without the company of her own family, she died in a matter of weeks. During those days, Ellen kept her company and remembers reading to her. Elizabeth's choice was *The Life of Henry Martyn*, an evangelical bestseller which told the story of the brilliant young mathematician who had given up a bright future to become a missionary in India with the Church Missionary Society, another agency the Clapham Sect were involved in. This memoir told of his moments of intense

3. Alldridge *The World's Workers*, 107.

loneliness, alongside his prayers for perseverance and his love for Christ. It described what must have seemed like a different world and Martyn's attempt to fit into it. He wore the local clothes, ate with his hands and smoked the shared pipe, as he spoke with Indian rulers and officials. His aim throughout was to translate the Bible and to encourage Indians to read it. These stories, read out loud in that desperately sad sickroom, lodged deep in Ellen's mind. They settled in her a conviction that 'Bible-work was the one work to which I had been called by God'.[4]

Learning to serve

The next fourteen years of Ellen's life were taken up with the Bible Society, alongside performing the expected niceties of life as a young woman in the early nineteenth century. She still enjoyed the popular books of the time, possibly including Hannah More's work, which remained popular for decades after her death in 1833. Wordsworth was certainly a favourite and she learned many of his poems by heart, longing to be able to meet this poet who recorded nature so tenderly. She carried on painting and spent time with her young siblings, watching them grow and eventually leave the family home to get married, writing little poems for them to celebrate their new start. Perhaps she was sad to see them go, knowing that she, the eldest, was left behind. We can't be sure whether she was frustrated by the limitations of her domestic life and if she, like other female poets and writers of the early nineteenth century, harboured resentment against the middle-class customs which were built around preserving a woman's reputation. We do know Ellen was pursuing her own

4. Alldridge, *The World's Workers*, 108.

voluntary work with great determination, and she did this with the support of her family and her church.

Worship was an important part of Ellen's life, taking up much of every Sunday. She was a member of a congregational church in Norwood, a few miles south of their home. You can still see the impressive Georgian building today, with its white stucco façade, symmetrical pillars and arched windows. It is now a childcare centre, but perhaps Ellen wouldn't be too disappointed by this if she saw the many new, ethnically diverse churches which have been planted in this area in the last few decades. The minister of her church was a scholarly man who picked up languages easily and whose preaching was full of practical application. From his example, she saw that she didn't have to discard her cultural interests or suppress her curiosity if she wanted follow Jesus seriously. In the Bible Society Committee likewise she was encouraged by others. It wasn't long before she was in charge of taking minutes and handling cash. And through these years she kept up her weekly rounds in her neighbourhood, getting to know people of all classes as she walked the streets and knocked on doors, persistently explaining their need to read the Scriptures.

This wasn't the only aspect of her Bible Society work. In 1845, when she was in her mid-thirties, she published a book of advice for young would-be Bible Collectors. That perhaps sounds dry, but it isn't. Her teaching comes through lively, easy-to-read stories of two girls rather unsurprisingly called Emily, new to the work, and Elizabeth, her more experienced friend. *The Bible Collectors* contains some of Ellen's personal memories as well as those of others, and serves as a poorly disguised tribute to the young girl who made such a mark on her. In the introduction,

Ellen tells her readers that the role of Bible Collector will suit girls who have 'leisure, piety and education', and it will bring them 'happiness', taking them into a 'sphere of usefulness'.[5] Her story shows some awareness of the resentment poorer people might feel towards such comfortably-off benefactors but that faith and compassion can cross class divides, hinting at the concern which sparked Ellen's later work. Just like Hannah More, Ellen sees that middle-class women have significant responsibilities and in the world. There are opportunities to offer practical help, and they can be involved in spreading the Word of God, just as much as a missionary who has gone far afield. This 'sphere of usefulness' was one which men could enter too, though they had their own committees, organised around the same goal and structure. But by keeping these wings of the local Bible Society's work separate, women were able to direct their work, according to what they understood of women's needs and desires, and use their own considerable skills of administration and publicity. Women weren't solely limited to local committees or single-sex organisations, as the early decades of the nineteenth century progressed, they were able to serve on some national boards, sharing with men the direction of the work of mission in this country.

It's certain that this kind of charity wasn't always welcomed, of course, either by those who were on the receiving end or those observing from a distance. Alongside books like Ellen's promoting the work of mission, there came writing attacking it. Charles Dickens, the famous nineteenth-century novelist

5. Ellen Ranyard, *The Bible Collectors* (Bagster and Sons, London: 1845), i, ii, 1.

mocks religious women in his great novel *Bleak House* (1852). His characters neglect their own families and are completely taken up with the needs of those they think need their help. Mrs Pardiggle goes from house to house reading the Bible to poor families, offering them tracts and support, which Dickens says is no help at all, and worse, insists that her own children spend their pocket money in helping the poor.[6] These scenes are funny, and do point out the dangers of middle-class Christian charity which could overlook the reasons for poverty and ignore individual need, but they are cutting and even cruel, skewering precisely some of the practices of Bible Society Collectors. Ellen was not deterred by criticism. Her persistent labours remind us that evangelism is rarely dramatic or quick and often will be rejected or misunderstood. Holding to God's promises, Ellen pressed on without shame to 'testify about our Lord' (2 Timothy 1:8).

6. Charles Dickens, *Bleak House* (Ticknor and Fields, Boston: 1867), 240.

8

New Discoveries, New Opportunities

In her twenties, Ellen, along with her parents, moved out of Nine Elms and into a more rural spot, again beside the River Thames. This was Swanscombe, a pretty village with a thirteenth-century church, woods and marshes by the river. Ellen's father took over an existing company, which used the chalk and clay produced in quarries nearby and shipped its goods out from the river wharves. The plant became the largest cement factory in Britain in the 1840s through his management, and the family's wealth was secured. Again, they found themselves living alongside their industry and so Ellen saw around her the reality of the working lives of the people she visited. Fog and smoke hung in the air and affected the health of the community, but factory work was perhaps better than rural labour. It continued year-round and wages were often better. By this point working hours had been limited by laws brought forward by evangelicals like Lord Shaftesbury; factory life, when available, could be a good prospect.

Ellen continued her Bible Society work and church meetings. Perhaps it was at one of these that she met her future husband, Benjamin Ranyard; he certainly shared her beliefs and supported her work.

Marrying in 1839, Ellen and Benjamin settled in Swanscombe and soon had a growing family. First there was Herbert, then three years later, Edith, followed by Arthur, after another three years, and then last of all Alice, a year after that. With four young children, life must have been very busy. But it seems that Benjamin was well off – he is described as 'of independent means' on the census, rather than having a particular job – and they had three female servants living with them, a cook, a housemaid and a nurse to help with the children. Although, by the standards of the day, they weren't living an extremely lavish life, they were certainly very comfortable. As the years hurtled by, Ellen threw herself into caring for and teaching her children, being part of her church and keeping up some of her Bible Society work. There was time amongst the busyness for holidays. Like the romantic poets she so admired, Ellen found real delight in wild places. When she'd been married for four years, she and Benjamin travelled the nearly six hundred miles to the Isle of Mull in the Hebrides. It is a long journey by car and ferry today, but in the 1830s it would have taken days of sea travel and rough carriage rides. Once they were there she marvelled at the caves and turbulent seas, being reminded of God's awesome power and her own smallness. She wrote about these trips in poems she collected and stored, adding to them poems for her children and for friends. Later she would have them published.

A passionate writer

When her children were in their late childhood, like so many mothers today, Ellen took on more work. She was approached by senior leaders at the Bible Society with a question. In 1854 it would be the fiftieth Jubilee of the organisation, and fittingly they wanted to mark it with a book about the Bible. Ellen's obvious ability and capacity for hard work, as well as her great commitment to the Society had marked her out and they knew that she would be able to produce what they were after. *The Book and Its Story: A Narrative for the Young* must have surpassed their expectations with its 500 pages of bouncy, detailed writing. It starts with Adam and briskly progresses through the Old Testament, with a focus both on what the ancient world was like and how God spoke to the people. Writing under her pseudonym L.N.R. as she always did, Ellen explains how hieroglyphs work and describes other early forms of writing. She talks with exciting detail about the construction of the pyramids. She describes the recent discoveries of statues and pillars, imported and displayed in the British Museum. You can see them still today: massive gateposts of Assyrian palaces and carved reliefs which narrate the histories of the Babylonian Empire, along with statues of half-man, half-beasts from Nineveh. Through all of these words and the accompanying line-drawn illustrations, Ellen is presenting the world of the Bible as real history, involving actual people and fascinating events.

We might question the colonialist attitudes of the period which made it seem natural for treasures found in the Arabian Peninsula and Africa to be uprooted for the benefit of Western Christians. But Ellen's purposes are clear. She wants to defend the reliability of the Scriptures in an age when biblical criticism was emerging. Scholars in Europe were questioning the accuracy of the Bible, often because they rejected the possibility of anything supernatural happening. At the same time, geologists were arguing that the earth was much older than the church had claimed. Although evangelicalism was flourishing in the 1850s, sceptical voices in society were growing louder by the year. Recent archaeological discoveries provided an opportunity to counter some of this doubt. Prior to the Bible Society's commission, Ellen had written a short book called *Nineveh and its Relics in the British Museum*, explaining these discoveries from a Christian perspective. Her children's book was another part of her a response to these challenges – it contained not only rip-roaring adventure but serious apologetics. The statues don't just tell of a lost culture but of the one God of history.

In the second half of *The Book and Its Story*, Ellen tells a narrative of church history which ranges through much of the world. She is keen to show that from the very first days of the church, Christians have been missionary-minded and the gospel has flourished in non-European settings. She writes about the persecution of early Christians in the Roman Empire in gory detail and she tells the story of the Coptic Church in Africa and of Armenian believers in the first millennium who travelled to India and beyond with the good news. She mentions early preachers in Britain, like Saint Columba, as well as those who spread the gospel amongst the Slavs and the Goths. She emphasises that everywhere the good news went, the Scriptures were translated into the local language. There might be a trace of Victorian imperialistic confidence in Ellen's attitude, but there is also a great concern that people all over the world can hear the Scriptures in their own tongue.

Ellen doesn't neglect theology as she tells this story. We hear about church councils and Reformation doctrine, detailing not only the prominent men who led these debates and movements but also key women, often unnamed, who played their part in cherishing the truth and passing on the good news. The Roman Empress Helena who built a church gets a mention, as does the wife of a man called Apollo, who couldn't be persuaded to leave the faith. There are English female martyrs from the fifteenth and sixteenth centuries and French nuns who copied the Scriptures. These vivid tales prepare the way for the final part of the book, the story of how the British and Foreign Bible Society continues this great work. There are facts and stories about every continent. The world is full of need as well as wonders, but the good news is making headway, Ellen claims. She ends with the exhortation:

> *Work together with God, who has said, 'My Word shall not return to me void; but it shall accomplish that which I please, and it shall prosper the thing, whereunto I sent it' (Isaiah 55:11).*[1]

The Book and Its Story is an extraordinary work. It displays Ellen's great ability to organise ideas and work hard. To produce 500 pages of small type, full of statistics from the present day and accurate historical and theological detail from the previous 2,000 and more years would be impressive for an academic today with digital libraries and search engines, but for a nineteenth-century

1. Ellen Ranyard, *The Book and Its Story: A Narrative For the Young* (Bagster, London: 1854), 482.

woman with no formal education, and four children, it is a marvel. That she managed to convey so such information in such a lively tone, making what could be dry genuinely gripping is even more impressive. Her book went into eight editions, selling incredibly well. Whether children read it all the way through, we can't be sure, but certainly it made its way into many homes, and if families only dipped into it, the book still did a good work.

The lull and the storm

Ellen's writing tasks were made easier by her move to London at about the time these projects began in earnest. Together, the family left the factories of Swanscombe for the newly developed, and rather grand area of Bloomsbury. The reason for the family's move, she made clear, was the children. She must have felt that they would benefit from a new, healthier and stimulating environment. This part of London, west of the old city centre, was becoming known as the place of the arts and education. The British Museum was based here and University College, London's first place of higher education, and the only college open to non-Anglicans (though still male-only) had been founded here twenty years before Ellen's move. Arthur, her second son went first to the college's attached high school and then to the college itself. He excelled in science and went on to have a brilliant career as an astronomer who is still remembered today.

In early 1849, Bedford College was founded, just round the corner from Ellen's house. It was the first place of higher education for girls in the country, offering teaching at degree level. A few years later, an attached girls' high school was opened to ensure students entered the college with the right level of knowledge. Here was an opportunity for Ellen's daughters Alice and Edith to have the formal education their mother had missed out on. The desire for seriousness in female education that we see in Hannah More's writing was beginning to bear fruit in this new generation, and it was being championed by many men and women of faith.

Not far from the peaceful retreat of Russell Square, 13 Hunter Street was a good address for the family. Their home no longer exists, and instead late-Victorian flats line the road. The house would probably have been like others from the early nineteenth century still standing in the area: terraced, four storeys high, possibly with a white stucco front and tall symmetrical windows to let in plenty of light. These houses display a restrained elegance. They are not mansions but very obviously comfortable places to live. Away from the river, with its busy traffic of barges and its stink of sewage and pollution, Bloomsbury had wide streets and leafy squares where children could safely play. Whilst the children were occupied, Ellen could spend time studying in the British Museum. Pillars, broken statues and huge stone temple carvings were beginning to fill its halls. She could also visit its library, crammed with shelf after shelf of books useful for her research. Ellen must have felt she was entering another world when she walked under the huge arched entrance, with its towering columns and Greek pediment, out of the noise and dirt of London's streets. Later in life, she said that this became her second home, a place she could write in peace.

That calm, however, was in contrast to the rest of her life. The move to London may have been for the educational and social opportunities it offered her children. Perhaps too it was for medical provision with University College Hospital nearby and plenty of well-trained doctors working in the capital. It is possible Ellen's daughters had been ill for a long time, perhaps from tuberculosis (commonly known as consumption) or it might have been they succumbed quickly in one of the devastating outbreaks of cholera which hit London in the mid-century. The records only show that first Edith died in 1859, then Alice, four years later. They were both sixteen.

The horror of this grief can't have been lessened by the high mortality rates of the period. No matter when or where one lives, the death of a child is devastating. The house must have been filled with the usual Victorian conventions of grief: black mourning clothes and quietness, treasured locks of hair set into jewellery and a renewed focus on what was eternal. Ellen was left with her husband and her younger son Arthur, the student. Herbert, her oldest child had at about this time set sail for Australia. We can only speculate what led the eldest son to take off for what would have been considered a wild backwater on the other side of the globe. Home must have been a very busy place as his mother's ministry grew, as well as being marked by grief and pain. It was also a centre of respectability and decorum, as well as religion. There was plenty of money, so he didn't have to work to earn his keep. Maybe this was all just too much for an energetic young man.

Herbert was married at the age of twenty-five in the town of Gundaroo, which was the centre of the gold rush a few years before. Seven years later, he is described as a 'squatter' in a local census, which means that he was grazing sheep on land beyond the boundaries of the white settlement. This was technically illegal, but a common thing to do for hardworking entrepreneurial men, often bringing great wealth. Herbert's place in Australian society became established and two decades later, he is mentioned in a newspaper as being part of a group meeting a Bishop touring the area. Ellen may, or may not have known about his adventures so different from his polite, semi-urban upbringing. And though he did become successful, it must have felt as though she and Benjamin had lost a third child. Herbert could have seemed to them like a prodigal who had abandoned his family and their God, leaving them alone in their grief and longing. We can only hope that some news of Herbert's church involvement later in his life trickled back to his watching parents and perhaps, as time went on, they learned to recognise in their wayward son some of the pioneering personality of his mother.

New opportunities

It is a brisk twenty-minute walk from Hunter Street to Seven Dials in the St Giles area. Today this destination is the heart of theatre land, where colourful posters and illuminated signs are emblazoned with names of celebrities and restaurants cater to well off tourists. In 1857, the narrow streets were squalid and gloomy, even in the June when Ellen made the trip with a retired doctor friend. She wrote later of the 'hot and fetid air', the broken windows and the 'dirty, haggard forms' who leant out of them.[2] In the street loitered women and children, their faces grimy and clothes in rags. The ground floor rooms were used as junk shops while whole families lived in the rooms above and in cellars beneath. In 1851 it was recorded that in one eight-room house, 107 people had their home. Behind the main street, tall,

2. Lizzie Alldridge, *The World's Workers*, 114.

broken-down houses were clustered around a courtyard, a small outside space, often housing a waterpump and 'privvy'. These often once grand homes had become the infamous 'rookeries' Charles Dickens described as 'compound[s] of sickening smells ... heaps of filth ... tumbling houses with their vile contents, animate and inanimate, slimily overflowing into the black road'.[3] Ellen was shocked by this extreme poverty. In her years of visiting in Nine Elms and Swanscombe she had been into poor homes. In *The Bible Collectors* she had written about those with little to eat and little to wear, but what she saw in this inner-city slum was of a different scale. Her compassion for the people swelled and her biggest concern was, 'How are these people in their countless courts and alleys supplied with the Bible?'[4]

When so many were destitute, that question might seem grossly insensitive to many today. It certainly did to some in the mid-nineteenth century, and it transparently reveals Ellen Ranyard's priority of spiritual rather than material welfare. The first ever British census of 1851 had alerted the church, if they weren't already aware, that, just as today, church going was a middle-class practice. Fifty-one per cent of British people could be found in church on any one Sunday, but the majority of these attenders were comfortably off; working-class people and slum dwellers were much less likely to attend worship. Like so many others, Ellen was troubled by this. In St Giles she had discovered a place where the older forms of parish support had broken down and Bible distribution had never begun. She would

3. Charles Dickens, '*On Duty with Inspector Field*', Household Words, 14th June, 1851.
4. Alldridge, *The World's Workers*, 115.

discover that this was the case in all the poorest areas of London and other industrial towns. Rapid urbanisation had brought streams of people from rural areas of Britain into cities. Irish people had fled poverty and famine, and Jews had sought refuge from persecution on the Continent in the packed courtyards of the East End. A system which relied on wealthy local benefactors and vicars knowing families and offering spiritual and material support couldn't operate in such a densely packed slums. The Bible Society's model of visiting, which Ellen knew so well, borrowed from this parish tradition and likewise wasn't suited to an area of such extreme poverty.

London certainly wasn't without people who cared for the poor and reached out with the gospel. The visionary Scot David Nasmith had established London City Mission in 1835 with the aim to 'to go to people in London and its vicinity, especially the poor ... in order to make them acquainted with the message of salvation through Jesus Christ, and to do them good by any means in the [workers'] power'.[5] He made particular attempts to reach out to needy women in the city, establishing a home for those leaving prostitution and a hostel for working women. His co-workers were not ready for such potentially reputation-risking enterprises and Nasmith left the organisation in 1837. For the next 150 years, the organisation stuck with paid male missionaries while allowing some women to volunteer alongside them in their work for the poorest communities. London City Mission's work was ground-breaking, reaching communities churches often didn't, but was less effective at connecting with

5. Quoted by Imogen Lee, 'Ragged Schools' (15 May 2014) www.bl.uk/romantics-and-victorians/articles/ragged-schools

women or the very poorest of all. Ellen's walk to Seven Dials prompted her to action with a new idea of how to meet these acute and sometimes hidden needs.

Two pioneers

First, she asked about Bibles. The vicar of St Giles told her that cheap Bibles could be had for a penny a week, but you had to visit the church to get these and the very poorest wouldn't venture into a place which seemed so respectable. She then spoke to the London City Mission missionary for the area who confirmed Ellen's opinion that a middle-class lady would never be able to gain entrance or win the trust of the people. The poor would be expecting hand-outs, scorn her delicacy or think she didn't understand. Ellen's simple but revolutionary idea was that a poor working-class woman could take Bibles into the courts and alleys of the area and make connections with the women who lived there. She wondered if Mr McCree the missionary knew of someone who might be willing to take up the challenge.

Ellen's brief biography tells us that when she asked this question, McCree had in his pocket a letter from a woman called Marian. Four years earlier he had given a Bible to her when she had stumbled into his mission hall to shelter from the rain. She had wanted to borrow a copy of *Uncle Tom's Cabin*, the popular anti-slavery story but for some reason felt impelled to ask for a Bible. She took and read it, and found herself changed. Marian was an orphan who had known extreme poverty growing up in St Giles. On her wedding day, she had no shoes or socks to wear, and though her husband worked, she had to eke out his income with earnings from making wax flowers and jewellery bags in their one room home. Still, despite the hardship, she loved her Bible and the truths it taught: her life was now safe in Jesus and she was loved by him with an unbreakable love. She wrote to McCree explaining that she now wanted to serve somehow: 'I wish to dedicate the time I have spare, not ... to the decent poor, but to the lost and degraded of my sex ... It will be enough for me that she will require my aid, such as washing her, and repairing her garments.'[6] Marian's desire was to be useful and to share the love of Christ. She seemed to be just the person that Ellen could work with.

So, the Bloomsbury lady and the St Giles working woman became partners in this enterprise. Ellen provided her with a bag of Bibles and support, and Marian went out into the alleys and courts, going further into the darkest corners of the area than even she had been before. The principle was just the same as with Bible collecting; those without Bibles would be given one, but they would have to pay for it, a penny a week. More than this, Marian was to make relationships. She went into plenty of rooms where families lived with piles of straw for a bed and only one or two broken chairs for furniture. The women all worked; they sold watercress or flowers in the markets, some traded in rabbit skins (you can imagine the stench), made paper boxes or firelighters, but they only earned enough for the most basic food items. Marian and Ellen could have given away clothes or vouchers for better food or fuel, but right at the start they decided that this would not be of long-term help for most. It would cause dependence and seem as though spiritual interest was being bought. Relationships would be tainted and the

6. Alldridge, *The World's Workers*, 119.

women would not learn to help themselves. Their priority had to be the Scriptures.

The response was remarkable. At the end of one month, seventy women had received Bibles, and a few weeks after this Marian invited eight of them to tea in her one room home. They drank tea and ate bread and butter while Marian spoke to them of what she had learned in the Bible. Then they shared their stories of life, struggles and faith. Over the next few months, the St Giles work grew. Marian was welcome in 200 homes and managed to sell more and more Bibles. As she became friends with these women she found ways she could help them practically. Those in great poverty, just as today, often were forced into eating poor quality but expensive food. Living hand to mouth, they either could not afford fuel to cook or had no utensils. Several families might share one room for their home, each taking a corner, so the fireplace had to be shared too. Generational poverty meant that cooking knowledge was not there to be handed down. They relied on the nineteenth century equivalent of take-aways. So, Marian and Ellen's plan was to sell a recipe for cheap soup and lend out saucepans it could be made in. They started clubs for sewing, so that women could make decent clothes for themselves and their families, paying a minimal amount for fabric and learning useful skills as they went. Mattresses and baby clothes were offered on the same basis. And this work gave the project its name: 'The Bible and Domestic Mission'.

Ellen was an irrepressible writer and so it was natural that she documented the work she and Marian were doing for others to learn about. She had been editing a monthly magazine for the Bible Society called, *The Book and its Mission*, so in this she inserted stories of the lives which were changing in St Giles. The information brought a financial response and the project snowballed. Marian's work had grown and was taking more and more time, so Ellen was now able to make sure she was paid a reasonable rate for her labours, 10 shillings a week, as well as to fund the increasing number of clubs which offered reduced costs for essentials. This move from voluntary to paid ministry shifted the whole enterprise, from a one-off experiment to a radical new model for women's service. Ellen concluded that she had found 'the missing link'; working-class women who could act as a powerful connector between privileged Christians and whole communities. They could go into places where the middle-class women and men of any kind had no access. They could bring the Scriptures and meaningful aid to those who were in great need of both. The next, and obvious step was to recruit more workers so that the Mission could be extended.

9

Light in Dark Places

One year after Marian first ventured out with her bag of Bibles, four more women joined the Mission. The work could now extend through the St Giles area and beyond it into the East End of the city. Each woman was given her own district, and a 'lady superintendent'; Ellen's plan was not solely about employing working-class women, but about partnership across the classes. Through the Bible Society, Ellen knew of many keen London ladies who wanted to serve and didn't need to be paid. Their gifts could be used in this new venture in a distinctive way. The ladies were to hold the financial reins of the district, managing accounts and ordering supplies. The missionaries, or 'Bible Women', as they quickly came to be called, then had all their time available for ministry, and most importantly, were able to act as free agents. The women they worked among knew that their visitor didn't dole out cash or charity directly, they had to ask their 'lady'. This clear demarcation of responsibilities underlined a rigid view of class. Middle-class women were in control and working-class women had to know their place. At the same time, this system made sure that the Bible Woman couldn't be leant on or pressurised for financial gifts; the focus of their visits was kept to developing relationships, practical advice and conversation about Christ. It also meant that women, some of whom had little or no experience in managing budgets and whose numeracy and literacy was limited, were not given a task they were not prepared for. If we ask why there wasn't a vision for equipping these keen workers from the start, the answer lies both in Ellen's social conservatism and also in the rapid growth of the organisation. She didn't anticipate how quickly the work would grow. In time, however, the rigidity did change, not initially through a deliberate policy shift, but through an absence of middle-class helpers.

One area of collaboration for the lady superintendent and the Bible Woman was the organisation of regular get togethers. 'Mothers' Meetings' were for cups of tea and Bible teaching, with the lady doing the formal speaking, and the Bible woman following this up, talking through the meaning of the message with individuals. Then there were sewing meetings and other types of lessons. Rooms had to be hired for these and supplies ordered. Often this meant borrowing the premises of mission or church halls, but sometimes rooms were privately hired as well. The centre for all the work remained, in these early years, Ellen's own home in Hunter Street.

Early on, Ellen realised that these women needed some training, so arranged that each should have three months teaching before any independent work was undertaken. It was important that the women had good Bible knowledge alongside being well informed about the Poor Laws and good domestic practice. There were opportunities to shadow an established

Bible Woman, to observe good practice and also to have a go at helping while with someone else. After three months, though, they were on their own, getting to know their carefully chosen district, and meeting the poor who lived in it.

Just under two years after Marian did her first visit, there were thirty-five Bible Women employed by the Mission; a year later in 1860, there were 135. After this, growth continued, although a little more slowly, and by 1870 there were 234 on the books. This boom in service didn't come out of nowhere. God was at work, and one of the ways he worked was through Ellen's extraordinary talent for publicity. Ellen moved from editing the Bible Society's magazine to writing one for the Mission, which she called *The Missing Link*. Stories from these were collected and brought out in book form in 1859 with another following in 1862. The focus in both of these books is her Bible Women and the women they work with, familiarising readers with the hardships of the slums: the overcrowding and unemployment, domestic violence and alcoholism. Then there is description of the dirt and damp of the homes, the ragged clothes and dirty faces of their inhabitants. Ellen's approach is sympathetic as she describes hardships which would have seemed hardly imaginable to her readers, as they do to today's readers. Some families existed on what they could pick out of rubbish piles, some items they could sell, like cat skins and broken pottery, other items they ate, like discarded vegetables and bones. Other slumdwellers were weavers or seamstresses, but more did unskilled repetitious and draining work. Ellen could understand why people so oppressed might look for comfort and security in short term pleasures, and why they resent, to begin with, the intervention of women who seem to know better. Ellen's understanding of the causes and results of poverty increased as she spent more time with those living in the slums. She saw how despair might lead to addiction and inadequate housing to illness. Many were impoverished by unstable, dangerous and poorly paid work.

Work was crucial in the nineteenth century because of the threat of the local workhouse. From 1834, instead of local parishes providing a small payment for those in extreme poverty, they worked together to form workhouses, places where anyone, whether disabled, elderly or workless for some other reason were housed. Those deemed to be fit and able were put to monotonous painful work such as picking apart ropes or crushing stone, or the domestic duties of the place, like washing or cooking, to pay for their support. Though the simple accommodation or plain food might still have been preferable to homelessness outside the walls, or even the previous small allowance parishes handed out, this new system was brutal in the splitting up of families and the lack of personal freedom. It felt as though poverty was being punished. Though occasionally, 'outside relief' might be provided for some needy individuals, in general, the only way to escape the workhouse was to provide for yourself.

Other Christians did try to address the cruelty of this system, as well as other social injustices. But Ellen wanted to provide immediate help, so trained her Bible Women to help the very poorest care for and support themselves. The modern proverb, 'If you give a man a fish, you feed him for a day. If you teach a man to fish, you feed him for a lifetime' fits with her ethos. It also fitted with the prevailing values of the time. In 1859, the fantastically named Samuel Smiles published his book *Self Help* and it was an instant bestseller; he instructed his readers how to climb up in the world through hard work and careful strategy. But although Ellen uses the language of self-help again and again in her work, her version of this idea was founded on God's grace empowering individuals to change. The Holy Spirit gave individuals power to say no to drink, so money was available for food and education. He changed hearts and so repaired marriages, meaning that mothers had a father's wage in addition to their own to pay rent and keep children clothed. He answered prayer and brought neighbours and church members to help each other. As God empowered Christians to live holy lives, he changed whole communities.

An expanding ministry

The rapid growth in the number of Bible Women being employed by the Mission, and the increasing number of areas of London being reached by their work was overwhelming. Ellen's task was to provide resources for the new recruits and to oversee the progress of the Mission. Bible Women needed connections with church leaders, rooms from which to work and training. There were communication issues to manage and the ongoing task of supporting staff, many of whom had been reached by Bible Women themselves. Ellen started her day at five in the morning, or sometimes earlier, and worked solidly at the headquarters in her own house, in the British Library reading room or, in later years, in nearby offices. She must have often been exhausted, but we find no trace of this in her writing. The stories she tells are all about her women, not herself. It would be wonderful to hear insights of her own personal experiences, her struggles and griefs, but the archives hold little of this. We are left to imagine her days, filled with meetings and paperwork and writing.

From the list of trustees of the organisation, we know that she was talking to the big names of the evangelical world. The chief trustee of the charity was the Earl of Shaftesbury, the most influential social reformer of the century. The Earl had successfully brought in laws to restrict the exploitation of women and children in industry, spearheaded the Ragged School Movement, worked for the compassionate treatment of the mentally ill and championed the provision of low-cost housing for workers. Other titled men and women were counted amongst key supporters. Ellen's zeal for the gospel had given her a confidence which meant that she could move between the Bible Women, their lady supervisors and these aristocratic patrons. In a society we tend to think of as starkly divided, Christian work was bringing the classes together, albeit in different roles. That unity was found too in the funding of the work. The very wealthy certainly contributed large amounts, but the sacrificial giving of ordinary people also allowed the Mission to keep on growing.

Although Ellen's books were a canny aid in her fund raising, she never makes a direct appeal for money. Some of them include summaries of the accounts of the Mission, revealing how donations were used, and also how money contributed by the poorest towards Bibles and into savings schemes was managed. Ellen relied on this transparency, coupled with the moving personal stories of her workers – not always successful or heroic – and their labours, as information which would bring in funds. And the money came in in extraordinary amounts. It is amazing to learn of the generosity of Christians, and especially Christian women in the nineteenth century. By the 1890s, a good number of families were spending more money on charitable giving than they did on anything else other than food, and the amount given nationally far exceeded the funding allocated to government poor relief. Much of this money was donated directly by women, showing how they had much more financial independence than we might assume. By the end of the century, for example, over half of the regular contributors to London City Mission were women. For missions focused on reaching women, women donated even more.

Ellen's many books were about far more than fundraising. The publicity she was gaining for the Mission was about maximising its reach. She wanted her readers to wake up to the needs in the country at large and to see how they could act to bring spiritual and social change. She sought to make connections between her largely middle-class readers and the women who worked for and were reached by the Mission, stirring up her readers to prayer and emotional engagement in the world outside their doors. In at least one book, she calls for even more than emotional or spiritual sympathy. You 'lovely butterflies', she writes, 'the purpose of your life has been spent on trifles'. With this shocking condemnation, Ellen challenges the comfortable ladies who lunch to find their 'life work'.[1] This is a no-holds-barred recruitment drive; the domestic and social whirl is just not enough, but neither is dabbling in charity or volunteering. Ellen argues her female readers have been given gifts and time to use for the blessing of others less fortunate than themselves, and they will be accountable to God for how they act.

Once husbands, children and family members are cared for, Ellen argues, reaching the lost and caring for the needy are

1. Ellen Ranyard, *Life Work, Or The Link and the Rivet* (James Nisbet and Co, London: 1861), 8-9.

the next priority. She calls women out of their homes to use their gifts, recognising that many women are bored and feel trapped by the constraints of the strict sex division of well-to-do society. She is clear: ministry can't be left to men; women must leave the private sphere and come into the 'sphere of usefulness'.[2] But she isn't radical in a way that would scare off her readers. Giving the example of the multi-talented wife of Proverbs 31, she talks about ministry as a type of mothering. She demonstrates how works of mercy in the community are really an extension of the work of a good housewife who should show concern for her servants and ensure a good living wage is paid. For women whose children are no longer little, they can use the skills they already have; single women can develop abilities they may need if later they marry. Her rallying cry is urgent, leaving no room for excuses, and centring on a beautiful picture of sisterhood:

> *The lord is calling out teachers for all classes of community, high and low, rich and poor ... It is no longer a day of priestly teaching only. Even outcasts are sent to outcasts, women to women, children to children. We are all one human family. Birth and death, sickness and grief have bound us together always, whether we would or not; and now the same book shall knit our hearts and kindle in us the love to Jesus which must show itself in true love to each other.*[2]

2. Ellen Ranyard, *Bible Collectors*, 1. This phrase is found throughout her works.
3. Ranyard, *Life Work*, 130.

Clearly, though, not enough women heeded this call – a few years later she was training experienced Bible Women to act as supervisors of their peers. Having served in the streets and homes, they were now able to take on the management of money and property. Their confidence in teaching Scripture was growing and they could run meetings on their own. The shape of the Mission was altering as it grew, developing in ways Ellen would never have anticipated; now working-class women were being equipped to manage their own ministries and be involved in financial decision making. It seems as though Ellen hadn't foreseen how empowering her scheme would be for the working classes, and the development wasn't easy for her to accept at first. She had to come to terms with the classes working alongside each other, not just as spiritual equals, but as equals in ability.

Going beyond

As soon as the Mission in London gathered momentum, it began to spread through Britain and beyond. City Missions, modelled on London City Mission, had already been started in other industrial centres and the Bible Society had its local associations all over the country, so the infrastructure existed for Ellen's model of women's ministry to be adopted easily. By 1862, a third of those volunteering with the Town and Missionary Scripture Readers Association were female; activity inspired in part by Ellen's work. Some churches began to set aside women as pastoral or evangelistic workers. Ellen annually supplied around ten trained Bible women to other cities and in 1871, nine women went into more rural areas. And of course, these local stations began to train their own women for the same kind of work. The concept of equipping working women for ministry was expanding, and Bible Women were going further still.

The middle of the nineteenth century saw a boom in missionary work around the globe. Women, both single and married, were answering the call and being trained to reach women who were kept secluded from society. In India and China, after puberty, girls lived in women's quarters, and the only way they and their children could hear of Christ was if Christian women learned their language and went to them. No doubt Ellen heard of this service and it inspired her work. Once the Bible Women's Mission was established, it fuelled this growing international movement of women's ministry.

Within the first ten years of the Bible Women's Mission, local replicas of this work had been founded in America, China and India, a direct result of Ellen's writing. A Southern Baptist missionary recorded that, 'My mother and my aunt were much interested in the account of Mrs Ranyard's work in London and my aunt sent $50 to be used in trying to secure Christian women who would visit the homes and try to bring the gospel to their own sex in China.'[4] There was also an even more direct influence, as Ellen's Mission was choosing to use its own funds to pay for the employment of Bible Women in other countries. In her record for 1871, Ellen tells her readers that there are twenty-one in the Middle East; three or four in India; one in each of France and the US and two in the Caribbean. Over

4. Quoted by Valerie Griffiths, *Biblewomen From London to China: The Transnational Aappropriation of a Female Mission Idea* Women's History Review Volume 17, 2008 - Issue 4.

fourteen years, the Mission had spent the equivalent of £206,000 on supporting local female missionaries abroad. It wasn't a brand that was being exported, or even an exact method. Ellen didn't attach her name to the work (that came after her death). She had simply developed and applied a simple strategy which others took and ran with: to train and support women to reach women like themselves.

Ellen had resisted for a number of years the most significant development in the history of the Mission. Over the first ten years, a rescue centre for prostitutes had been established along with an orphanage. An ambitious plan of Marian's, the first ever Bible Woman, to create a safe, cheap hostel for single working women had been a great success, keeping young and vulnerable women away from exploitative landlords. But when suggestions were made to train some of her Bible Women as nurses, Ellen resisted. Female nursing had become big news in the mid-1850s when Florence Nightingale took a band of trained nurses out during the Crimean War to put chaotic military hospitals in order. She quickly became a national heroine, with memorabilia being produced to celebrate her achievements even before she had returned home. Before this, professional nursing was seen as employment of last resort, work for those who couldn't or wouldn't do another job. It was fine for ladies to care for their own relatives, but to get their own hands dirty for money, was beyond the pale. Nightingale had shown the public that nursing could be a respectable job for middle-class women.

Ellen feared training her workers up as nurses would be a distraction from the central goal of getting the gospel out. For her, physical needs just couldn't be allowed to take the place of the even more urgent spiritual needs of the poor. Alongside this was her anti-Catholicism. Where nursing wasn't being done badly by the roughest sorts, it was mostly being done by Catholic or high church religious orders. Ellen didn't want her female workers to seem like these Sisters. Her attitudes might seem harsh, but her knowledge of the slums had shown her the worst of superstitious Catholic traditions. In the East End, Irish and European immigrants would cling to their Catholic identity, warned away from the Bible Women's help by their priests and so remained ignorant of the Bible and the hope it offered. Lastly there came a practical consideration. The Mission would need another level of administration, accommodation and supplies if it was going to undertake the task of providing nursing care seriously.

Once Ellen and her team became convinced that nursing was the way ahead, however, they embraced it wholeheartedly with a clear vision, establishing this new ministry in 1868. In her book *Nurses for the Needy*, written ten years later, she describes their work. It is a fulfilment of Christ's command, she says, quoting the Scriptures: 'Defend the poor and fatherless. Show mercy to the afflicted and the needy. Do as you would be done by, if you lay sick and helpless in those miserable rooms!'[5] Her nurses all started as Bible Women, taking the usual three months of teaching and shadowing of experienced workers. Some would stay in this role, others would go on to be trained in a hospital for another three months, watching operations, dressing wounds and learning about hygiene, followed by some additional

5. Ellen Ranyard, *Nurses for the Needy or Bible-Women Nurses in the Homes of the London Poor* (James Nisbet, London: 1875), 3.

weeks in a maternity unit. Along with a very strong stomach, the qualifications to be trained were 'truthfulness, honesty and kindliness of heart, as well as true piety'.[6]

This is a very long way from the arduous three years of university study a nurse must undertake today, with exams and dissertations as well as practical work experience, but of course, medicine was very different in the nineteenth century. Without anaesthesia, antibiotics, cancer treatments apart from simple surgery, or much pain relief beyond opium, many ill people lived with significant amounts of discomfort and distress. Hospital care was expensive, and often pointless; home was where most sick people stayed. But if your home was a damp cellar or an overcrowded, dirty room, your chances of recovery would be slim, and so your poverty would increase. A visit from a Bible Nurse, with her simple training, could then make all the difference. She could clean and dress wounds so that they could heal, lift you to prevent bed sores, wash you and change your bedding. And alongside this came words of comfort and Bible reading. Ellen tells the story of a woman whose burns from a household accident had become infected and wouldn't heal. She couldn't afford clean bandages or treatment. The pain was overwhelming and the smell was rank. She couldn't earn money or take care of her home or her children. This had gone on for months before the Bible Nurse arrived. Day by day the nurse came and cleaned the wounds, dressing them gently with sterile cloths. The infections subsided and they began to heal. The woman's spirits lifted and she was able to make some order around her home. And while all this happened, the Bible Nurse was able to speak of Jesus.

6. Ranyard, *Nurses*, 300.

Other nurses tended those who were dying or took care of new mothers. They were in great demand because all their services were free. They worked with doctors and hospitals, referring patients and receiving advice. In keeping with the self-help ethos of the Mission, the nurses aimed to pass on their skills to families of sufferers and to give health advice so that disease could be prevented. They were, in fact, the first ever District Nurses, very similar to those who care for the elderly and chronically or terminally ill today in the UK. Their service was so valued that it lasted nearly a century, going through several changes until in 1965 their work was absorbed into the London Boroughs' District Nursing Service. The nursing arm of the organisation had become separated from the mission side well before this, however. There were still Bible Women in the early twentieth century, but gradually numbers decreased. By the twenty-first century, all that is left of Ellen Ranyard's work is a nursing home in the East End of London bearing her name but owned and run by a consortium.

It tempting to wonder what Ellen would have made of this legacy. She died in 1879, aged sixty-nine. A photograph of her in old age shows a determined looking woman, with fussy ringlets and bundled up, as Victorian ladies were, in lace cap, ribbons and shawl. She has left little personal record of her experiences running a rapidly expanding organisation which made such a wide and deep impact – on the lives of individuals as well as on the church. Maybe she would be sad that her Mission seems to have disappeared, but more likely she would be able to celebrate the alleviation of much of the extreme poverty in London along with the growth of other mission agencies which continue to train women of all backgrounds to reach marginalised women.

She would certainly be thrilled to see the Bible still being handed out and shared by Londoners in all kinds of ways. The vast numbers of words she wrote may only be of interest to historians now, but her central ideas are worth remembering. If Hannah More was passionate about women's education and saw a role for women in teaching and activism, Ellen Ranyard went further in her explicit encouragement of women into Bible teaching and paid Christian service. Using multiple examples from the Bible she knew so well, she insisted that:

> *The highways and byways need their 'Deborahs' – their mothers in Israel – and there is work unending for the handmaids of the lord 'on whom he shall pour out in these days ... his spirit!'*[7]

While Ellen was clear that it was unscriptural for women to address mixed audiences, she knew that they 'had been given the gift of utterance', and whether through writing, public speaking or in one-to-one conversations they were being called by God to reach and build up others beyond the walls of their own homes.[8] The many eminent men and church leaders she partnered with gladly accepted and encouraged this mission. Ellen's work demonstrates for us how central strong women were to the growth and health of the evangelical church in the nineteenth century, and reminds us that the courageous service of 'handmaidens' and 'Deborahs' is needed today.

---

7. Ranyard, *Life Work*, 271.
8. Ranyard, *Life Work*, 271.

A Voice in the Wilderness

JOSEPHINE BUTLER,

1828-1906

10

Privilege and Pain

If any of the women in this book had a privileged childhood, it was Josephine Butler. Family wealth and stability set her up for an easy, conventional adulthood. She could have settled into a straightforward, good life, but she chose instead difficulty and risk. Josephine placed herself beside some of the weakest and most scorned women in society and used her privilege to fight for their protection. Because of this fight, Josephine is a fairly well-known figure in the story of women's rights, but not so many know that Christ was the source of her strength and motivation.

Josephine was born into the Grey family in 1828 when Hannah More was an old woman and Ellen Ranyard was at the end of her teenage years. The seventh child of loving, wealthy parents, Josephine had great freedom growing up. They were part of the aristocratic Grey line, and for her first seven years, they lived in a house in the north of England on the family estates which her father managed, close to the border with Scotland. After this, they moved about fifty miles south to the village of Dilston, in what is now County Durham. Her father had been asked to run the vast estate belonging to Greenwich Hospital which stretched across the Pennine Hills of Northumberland and into Cumbria. He built a large and beautiful house for the family, looking out over the romantic ruins of Dilston Castle. In later years, Josephine treasured her memories of 'the bright, large family circle and the kind and hospitable character of its master and mistress' as well as the surroundings: the 'wild wood paths and beds of ferns … slender birch trees … the dry bed of a mountain stream'.[1] It was an idyllic place to grow up. There she could ride her pony, Apple Grey, exploring the high valleys with her favourite sister Hatty, who was just two years younger, and play with her other siblings, acting out the adventure stories their mother read to them. The Grey children accumulated pets, including ferrets, wild cats and even owls. They went on walks and did their lessons together. In winter the girls joined their brothers and local gentry for the excitement of hunting, chasing over hedges and through fields in all weathers. But often Josephine hid away by herself to play the piano or to think. Suffering from asthma, she wasn't as physically strong as the others and she had a reflective mind, often overwhelmed with nagging thoughts and sadness.

Josephine never wrote an autobiography, but in later years, she composed a memoir of her father's life. In this long book she reveals not only the family's deep connections with the Northumbrian landscape, but the ties they had to the wider world and their sense of responsibility to others. There was

1. Josephine Butler, *Memoir of John Grey of Dilston* (Edmonston and Douglas, Edinburgh: 1869), 189.

much in family conversation to make her think hard. Her father's cousin was the Prime Minister Charles Grey, the 2nd Earl Grey, who led a Whig government between 1830 to 1834. It was under his leadership that the ownership of slaves in British territories was made illegal. Josephine's father, John, was himself deeply involved in the abolition campaign, being a close friend of Thomas Clarkson, William Wilberforce's fellow campaigner. Once this battle was won, he joined the fight against enslavement in the Americas. Fights for parliamentary reform raged and Lord Shaftesbury's bills sort to protect workers in factories and mines. We might imagine that Victorian children were always shielded from such vicious realities of life, but John Grey didn't hold back. He felt it his duty to educate them about inequality and so inspire them to action. Josephine learned of the cruel punishments inflicted on fellow human beings, of how their children were snatched away from their mothers and how women endured relentless sexual exploitation. Josephine knew that though her family was happy and secure, she lived in a world of sin.

Wrestling with God

Biographers tell us of the Grey family's evangelicalism. Their lives were occupied by doing good to those around them and centred on God's Word. The first public speech John Grey gave was for the Bible Society. Close to home there were schools to be established, modernisation of farming methods to be overseen, and poverty to be averted. John Grey rode long distances and laboured hard to care for the many acres entrusted to him, and more, for the people who depended on this land. By the end of his working life he was delighted that all his workers were literate and all their children attending school. Josephine's mother, Hannah, was equally spiritually minded. A story was handed down that as a baby she had been blessed by John Wesley, though he had died a couple of years before her birth, so it was clearly a mis-remembrance! Her family roots were not so well-to-do as John's; her distant forebears were Huguenots, French Protestant refugees, but her parents had been Moravians, like Rebecca Protten. She had been brought up with a strong emphasis on the Bible, prayer and heart religion. Together, John and Hannah would have made sure that daily family worship was prioritised in their home, for servants as well as children, and every Sunday they walked the one and a half miles together, crossing the River Tyne to St Andrew's Church in Corbridge.

Looking back on her church experience later in life, Josephine remembered best those times when her nurse Nancy took her and Hatty to a Methodist Chapel her father had built for his workers. The earnestness of the people and the simplicity of their worship struck Josephine powerfully. Later in childhood a governess took her to revival meetings run by the Irvingite sect.[2] There was something about these gatherings which gave Josephine a conviction that the Christian God was powerfully able to reveal himself and to answer prayer; he was a God of love who could be known personally. From childhood she knew that faith must be immediate and demanding; dry and formal worship was worse than nothing. More than that, she found that the gospel, simply preached, had potential to bring together people of different classes, and to bring hope and true transformation. It is no wonder that she said of herself when an

2. This was an early Pentecostal movement led by Scottish clergyman Edward Irving (1792 – 1834).

old woman, 'I was brought up Wesleyan'; the atmosphere of her home was one of heart religion.[3]

Yet, despite her faith, or perhaps because of it, Josephine entered a period of intense struggle when she was in her late teens. Family games around the fire in winter, the house with its 'door which stood wide open, as if to welcome all comers, through the livelong summer day', and the beauty of the fells, weren't enough to stop her agonies.[4] She wrote in later life of how she ran away into the woods, where 'kneeling on the ground, I used to shriek to God to come and deliver'.[5] Her heart was in extreme pain, not out of self-pity, but for grief at the 'inequalities, injustices and cruelties in the world'.[6] The horrors of enslavement, and the exploitation of souls closer to home in the mills and factories of the north, mixed with grief within her own family: her older brother John had been lost at sea and a baby sister, Ellie, died of typhus when Josephine was just five years old. Perhaps even more distressing was a visit to Ireland around this time when she saw, heard and smelt the pain and stench of the potato famine. How could the God of love stay silent when crops rotted in fields and starving, skeletal families were evicted from hovels? How could this God be known in a world of pain? Josephine refused easy answers and attractive distractions and in her darkness, she wrestled with her thoughts.

---

3. From Josephine's letter to Miss Jane Priestman in 1883. Quoted by Jane Jordan, *Josephine Butler* (John Murray, London: 2001), 16.
4. Butler, *Memoir of John Grey*, 161.
5. George and Lucy Johnson, ed., *Josephine Butler, An Autobiographical Memoir* (J.W. Arrowsmith, Bristol: 1909), 180.
6. Butler, *Memoir of John Grey*, 161.

This period of struggle did end, though deep grief for the pain in the world would frequently overshadow her in adult life. Josephine's comfort came from Christ. In a felt experience of Christ's nearness and peace she found 'the light and hope and guidance which He never denies to them who seek and ask and knock, and which become for them as "an anchor of the soul, sure and steadfast"'.[7] While Josephine in her later years rejected some doctrines as too difficult, she never lost her conviction that God would judge sin and offered forgiveness to all who would trust in his Son. She believed that Christ had died for the sins of the world and that the Bible was truly his Word, revealing his love and compassion. Every day of her life she spent some time reading the Bible, she knew many passages by heart and her writings are saturated with its truths, whether in direct reference or as the basis for her arguments. And as she read, she also prayed, kneeling where she was, on her own or with others, sometimes for hours on end. Facing deeply distressing horrors, she was convinced that her God would hear and act on behalf of his people.

Growing up

All around Josephine were women who loved God and were bright and resilient. Not only did her nurse and governess model Christ to her, but so did her relatives. Her mother, Hannah, had to care for the large family and also manage the substantial household during her husband's frequent trips away. There may have been love and freedom, but idleness was not encouraged. More daring was Josephine's Aunt Margaretta, who lived just a

7. Johnson, ed., *Josephine Butler*, 16.

few miles away in Newcastle. This woman of deep Christian faith was heavily involved with political activism, organising protest through letter writing and petitions. At one time she dressed as a boy to listen to a debate in Parliament from the observers' gallery, then prohibited to women. It is hard not to think of her when we learn of Josephine's own visits to parliament to lobby politicians and her attendance in the new women's gallery when important votes were taking place.

Despite all this, the Grey family's approach to their girls' education was not ambitious. Josephine's mother read books to the children and governesses must have instilled some knowledge. She and Hatty were sent to school in Newcastle for two years as well, but none of this was enough to allow her to feel she had anything like the resources of knowledge possessed by the men and some women she would meet later in life. This brought her frustration. The developments in women's education which Ellen Ranyard saw in London had not spread to the hills of Northumberland. Her parents made sure that Josephine's Christian faith was nourished, her musical abilities nurtured and her social conscience was fired but, just as for her sisters, they hoped only for a good marriage and motherhood. Perhaps one reason for this aim was the great love the Grey parents found in each other. Their letters are full of tender respect and delight, speaking of their joy in family life. When Hannah was away from home, John wrote to his 'beloved wife', 'why should I always wish for your understanding and approbation [approval] of my matters, I wonder? You are a person of great influence over my weak mind!'[8] Later, Hannah, when away on

8. Butler, *Memoir of John Grey*, 160.

her own, wrote with evident pride: 'I often think of you all, and I think I see the little party round the oak table at tea when papa's day's work is over and he has the ready joke to each.'[9] It was no wonder that the whole family sought comfort in domesticity.

Josephine saw three of her sisters married when she was in her teens. First, Tully married a banker, then Eliza married a surgeon; last, Fanny got married to a vicar. Josephine must have watched and wondered when her turn would come. There were plenty of opportunities to meet eligible young men at social events, whether hunting, dances or gatherings with other comfortably off families. All the girls were beauties and not short of admirers. In the early paintings of Josephine we can still see her attractive poise, wavy chestnut hair and strong, even features. Much later, it was said of her that she was the most beautiful woman in London, though perhaps this admirer was influenced by her passionate advocacy and fearlessness, seeing her almost as a superhuman, and perhaps even terrifying, force.

Whether George Butler saw this at first, we can't say. When he met Josephine she was around twenty and he was a young Classics lecturer at nearby Durham University. They were probably introduced through Josephine's new brother-in-law, who was pursuing graduate studies there. It is easy to see why she would be attracted to George. Nine years older than Josephine, he was handsome and confident, an academic all-rounder with an interest in art as well as classical literature. He was a keen sportsman, representing the university at cricket, playing tennis in summer and enjoying skating on frozen rivers and running with hounds in winter. He even saved the life of a swimmer who

9. Butler, *Memoir of John Grey*, 171.

had got into trouble in the Thames. His father was a bishop, a highly educated man who longed for his bright son to become a clergyman. George resisted this, feeling it wasn't his calling despite his strong personal faith. One writer reasons that this was, in part, because of the high church movement sweeping through the Church of England. George wanted to steer clear of a church establishment which was becoming focused on ritual and display, and yearned instead for heart devotion to the Lord.[10] It would be hard to imagine a better match for Josephine.

Not long after the two were introduced, love letters began to flow between them and the two families met formally. In 1850, George moved to Oxford to take up the post of Public Examiner; their letters continued, Josephine writing of picnics, birdsong and flowers, while George wrote of his work and books. Three years later in January 1852 – the same year that Ellen Ranyard published *The Book and Its Story* – they were married with great festivities. The twenty-four-year-old Josephine wore white, with orange blossom in her hair and a long veil. There was dancing, a bonfire and fireworks. Visitors travelled by train from far afield and servants were treated to their own party. After the honeymoon, the couple moved to a three-storey terraced house on the High Street of Oxford. Then, as now, 'The High' in Oxford was a busy thoroughfare, with students and academics hurrying to lectures and tutorials; shoppers and tradespeople going about their business. Their house is now a restaurant, but you can still see the Georgian sash windows above the entrance and appreciate how this home must have felt a strange place to the young bride, used to wandering freely out of her door into

10. Jordan, *Josephine Butler*, 28.

trackless woodland. Oxford, for Josephine, was to be a place of mixed experiences; there were many exciting opportunities, but she found amidst these an atmosphere of oppression.

New discoveries

George's income wasn't generous – being an examiner was a junior post – but they had a small allowance from his father and probably an income from her father too, as was common for daughters of the gentry. There was no need for her to earn money and, with only had a small household to run, Josephine could enjoy a new kind of freedom. George was a moderniser, wanting to bring into the university the study of Art and Geography, previously thought to be only suitable for schoolchildren or women. He shared his work with Josephine and her intellectual confidence grew; through George her world was expanding. Josephine attended lectures and discussed them with him. Together they copied drawings and created maps to illustrate his lectures. They also studied literature together in the Bodleian Library, reading medieval works in Italian and Middle English. Josephine proudly wrote, 'in everything in which I was competent to do … it was my happiness to work with him'.[11] There was leisure time together too, riding out of the city to explore woodlands and hills, listening to the nightingale which sung in their small garden and playing Beethoven sonatas; she had received both a piano and a pony as wedding gifts! To add to their evident joy, Josephine became pregnant and just eleven months after their wedding gave birth to a healthy little boy.

11.Josephine Butler, *Recollections of George Butler* (Arrowsmith, Bristol: 1896), 93.

Through these early years, a counter-current ran which disturbed Josephine's contentment. Oxford was a male-dominated environment. There were no female students at this point,[12] and Fellows – which included most but not all academics – could not be married men. Josephine quickly became a popular hostess; George's colleagues could come away from their perhaps spartan College rooms into an elegant environment where a woman's presence seemed to sweeten the all-male competition and bravado. There would be music, Josephine on the piano of course, and others joining in, as well as conversation, sometimes witty, sometimes serious. As the only woman, Josephine often 'sat silent', lacking the training, and perhaps the confidence, to put ideas into words. At times as she listened her heart was 'sore' because of observations she heard and couldn't answer.[13]

Josephine wrote later of some of the conversations which disturbed her and which set the direction of the rest of her life. On one occasion men described a painting of a praying woman as 'insipid', suggesting that religious women were weak and indulgent; Josephine was incensed by their ignorance of women and prayer.[14] Another debate centred on Mrs Gaskell's novel *Ruth*, published in 1853. The book had generated controversy through its sympathetic portrayal of the central character. Ruth was an orphan who, lacking parental care or guidance, is seduced by the wealthy Mr Bellingham. She realises too late that he is cruel and self-interested, and he abandons her. Her reputation has been

12. Exams were only opened to girls in 1870 and lectures for women didn't begin until 1873.
13. Butler, *Recollections of George Butler*, 94.
14. Butler, *Recollections of George Butler*, 96.

ruined by living with a man when unmarried, and now she is pregnant. A kind clergyman takes her in and provides her with work, and Ruth discovers a type of redemption: she is accepted by God and able to lead her illegitimate son to him. In this way, Mrs Gaskell was showing that a 'fallen woman' was a victim, not a temptress, and demonstrates that shame and stigma can be overturned. She was part of a growing movement among writers, artists and churches to show mercy towards women abandoned or exploited by men. Josephine's Oxford visitors weren't convinced, however, and dismissed the book. Like many in society, they thought Ruth, and all the real women she represented, rather than her seducer was to blame.

There was perhaps no wonder that this attitude was so prevalent in Oxford. The rule of chastity for academics and the large numbers of unsupervised young men meant that prostitution and secret relationships were rife in the town. A stone's throw from the Butler's home on the High was Carfax, a notorious pick-up spot at night. A double standard which exonerated powerful men and blamed women suited this city particularly well. Josephine wasn't unaware of this, and it was brought home to her in another heart-breaking conversation. Distressed by the pregnancy of 'a very young girl' who had been seduced by a university Fellow, Josephine spoke to one of George's friends, a senior clergyman and academic. He advised her to keep quiet; it was 'dangerous to arouse a sleeping lion', the man's career was too important.[15] Despite having a woman on the throne, significant developments in female education and the strength of the evangelical church, many in Victorian society

15. Butler, *Recollections of George Butler*, 96.

held attitudes which were far removed from the compassion Christ showed. Facing this misogyny, Josephine wrote that her heart was 'in revolt' and that she suffered 'as only God and the faithful companion of my life will know'.[16] Just as in her teenage years, she suffered through the pain of others, refusing to take the easy option and turn aside.

Her deep grief at such hypocrisy led both George and Josephine to action. She read of a young girl who had been seduced and then abandoned when pregnant, and in despair arising from her extreme poverty she had killed her baby. This girl was being held in Newgate Prison. Josephine decided to get involved; she wanted to 'speak to her ... of God who saw the injustice done and who cared for her'.[17] George's suggestion was even more courageous, and she embraced it. Mirroring the plot of *Ruth*, they decided to offer a home and a job to the girl once her sentence was over. She became their servant, a member of the household, and in this act of radical hospitality Josephine's ministry of caring for the sexually exploited had begun.

---

16. Butler, *Recollections of George Butler*, 96.
17. Butler, *Recollections of George Butler*, 97.

11

Deeper Still

In these Oxford years, George was busy, seeking to develop his career. The role of examiner was temporary and limited. He needed something more established. At the same time, he was a man of integrity and ideas, wanting to use his giftings for good and bring changes to an archaic academic world, so he didn't fit easily into the dusty structures of the university. Though he had earlier resisted his father's encouragement to serving in the church, he now took this step and was ordained in the Church of England. To Josephine this felt momentous, for herself, as much as for George. She felt herself so united to him that his calling seemed as if it were hers, corresponding to her desire for wholehearted devotion to Christ. For George, this meant a new role; he took on the work of curate at St Giles Church in central Oxford. In this city of ideas, where both high church advocates and liberal critics were popular, George defended Scripture as the reliable Word of God and through his preaching called parishioners to a simple trust in Christ.

When George or Josephine travelled from home in these early years of marriage, letters flowed between them. These letters demonstrate how much they relied on each other for spiritual support and how united they were in their faith. They pointed each other to Bible texts and wrote about their experiences of prayer. George observed:

> *I think we are well fitted to help each other. No words can express what you are to me. I may be able to cheer you and ... by means of possessing greater physical strength ... I may be enabled to help you in the years to come, to carry out your plans which may under His blessing do some good.*[1]

These words were fulfilled; George's tireless sometimes public, sometimes private support was essential to Josephine's later mission. And these words exemplify, too, the complementarian nature of their marriage. Each served the other in a particular way, accepting their differences. George was the head of the household which meant he sacrificed himself so that Josephine might obey Christ and grow to be more like her Lord.

George combined his pastoral role at St Giles with ongoing study projects and, realising that an academic career was no longer possible, a plan to establish a new private boarding house for undergraduates. This last project had a two-fold aim. It would allow the family a more secure footing in Oxford, providing both a comfortable family home and an income, as well as giving students the opportunity to live in cheaper accommodation outside of college precincts. To this end the family moved into

1. Butler, *George Butler*, 122.

'Butler Hall' on St Giles Street in 1854, a large sandstone fronted house, and not long after their second child Arthur (known by his second name Stanley) was born. Josephine was settled there at first with her two sons, but by autumn 1856, around the time that Ellen Ranyard's work in London was beginning, she was pregnant again and seriously ill. Her doctor insisted that her sickness was brought on by the damp air and floods in Oxford but made worse by her 'spiritual and intellectual being'.[2] She seems to have been depressed, frustrated by her physical and spiritual limitations and burdened by the hypocrisy she'd discovered in society around her. It is highly likely that her pregnancies also contributed to these physical and mental health issues. The only hope, George was told, was to get out of Oxford, which meant relinquishing his academic ambitions. He gave it all up gladly for her.

After a time of convalescence in the warmer environment of Bristol where a third son Charlie was born, George found work not far away as assistant headmaster of Cheltenham College. Although an academic climb down, it suited his all-round talents and pastoral heart well. In this smaller town, George could shine. There was job security and a splendid, eight-bedroom home which went with the job. Before long, in 1859, their last child was born to thirty-one-year-old Josephine, a little girl they named Evangeline – Eva for short. Life was now very full in the Grey household. Two of Josephine's sisters lived nearby and with their families were frequent visitors to the house. During term-time George was engaged with school business, including caring for thirty boarders, but he still had time for songs and games

2. Quoted by Jordan, *Josephine Butler*, 47.

with his own little ones and there were summer trips up to the Lake District and Northumberland, reviving for Josephine very happy memories of courtship and childhood. Her depression seemed over, though she continued to suffer bouts of ill health. But, in 1864, just as the family had returned from holiday an accident occurred which would overshadow the remainder of their lives.

Loss and gain

The Cheltenham house was handsome and solidly built. A grand staircase complete with iron balustrade and polished mahogany rail ran up from the large hall to the third-storey bedrooms. On the evening of 20 August, five-year-old Eva was at the top of the stairs, having left her governess in the schoolroom and was going to say goodnight to her parents downstairs. Like any youngest child, she wanted to copy her older siblings and so she began to slide down the banister. In one awful moment, she fell, landing on the stone floor forty feet below. Some reports say her seven-year-old brother Charlie saw the event. At any rate George, on hearing the cry of a servant rushed out of the drawing room and picked up his daughter. She lived for about three hours following the fall but never regained consciousness.

It is hard to overestimate the impact of this loss on the family. Eva had been the darling of the family and in their memories became a perfect child. Josephine was haunted by the last words she had spoken to her only daughter who wanted to show her a caterpillar in a box: 'Now trot away, for I am late for tea.'[3] Worse was the memory of the actual fall which would revisit

---

3. Butler, *George Butler*, 154.

her every day for the rest of her life: 'The fall, the sudden cry, the silence.'[4] The family comforted themselves with thoughts of Eva's childlike faith and the Lord's love for little ones. They were convinced that they would meet her again; that God cared for them in their grief and that he had good plans for them but still, of course, they were plunged into a morass of sorrow. By winter, Josephine's health had given way, overburdened by her sadness and fears. In spring 1865, nine months after the accident, she wrote of the only way she could manage her intense feelings: 'I just have to put my hand in Christ's and ask Him to put His hand on my heart & keep it quiet.'[5] He answered her prayers, not by silencing her grief, but by expanding it, giving her a deep empathy for other sufferers and driving her to passionate intercession. The concern for exploited women which had so stirred her in Oxford returned, and she prayed:

> *That Christ will come quickly and deliver for ever the poor groaning world: the slaves from all their woes ... and slaves of lust in our own land, the poor women who are driven as sheep to the slaughter into the slave market of London.*[6]

Though one biographer sees that this is an unnatural response to bereavement, it fits the pattern of Christian discipleship. Josephine was groaning out a Romans 8:12-27 kind of prayer; the way we should all pray in our losses, however small or large.

---

4. Butler, *George Butler*, 154.
5. From Josephine Butler's 'Private Thoughts' spiritual journal, held in the National Records Office, pp.24, 37, quoted by Jordan, *Josephine Butler*, 64-65.
6. Jordan, *Josephine Butler*, 64-6.

God would build his kingdom through her faithful, prayer-filled response to loss.

The link in Josephine's prayer between those enslaved still in the southern states of America and prostitution is fascinating. As we've seen in the stories of Rebecca Protten and Hannah More, evangelicals had come to see slavery as a national shame and the campaign for abolition as an essential battle. By using the same language to describe both, Josephine implies that there is a new battle to be fought and a new group of people to be emancipated. This time, however, the injustice was happening on home territory.

Josephine Butler wasn't the first to be deeply concerned about the fate of socially shamed 'fallen women', a category which included prostitutes and women who were sexually active while unmarried – though it is worth remembering that many working-class women did secretly have sex with sweethearts but got married when they fell pregnant. Not only had Mrs Gaskell made this a theme of *Ruth* in 1853, but in *Mary Barton* (1848) she had shown the seduction and abandonment of a girl who had then been driven into prostitution. More than a hundred years before, the artist Hogarth had depicted a similar story of corruption in 'A Harlot's Progress', and Pre-Raphaelite painters, some of whom the Butlers knew personally, produced moving pictures which hinted at the morally complex situations of seduced women in the 1850s and 60s. Charles Dickens repeatedly depicted sympathetic 'fallen women' characters in his novels, just as Victor Hugo did in *Les Misérables*. Victorian people were well aware of the dangers of unscrupulous men and the vulnerability of unprotected young women, the stereotype of the suffering prostitute was all around. But could these women, once fallen, return to decent society? And who was to blame for their fall?

Although our culture usually imagines churches, especially those in the Victorian period, as judgemental and perpetuating shame, most often in the nineteenth century it was Christians reaching out to prostitutes and offering them a route away from exploitation. As Ellen Ranyard's mission grew, she established a refuge for prostitutes who wanted to leave the streets, and her dormitory for young working women was a preventative measure, keeping the cost of living low so that they wouldn't be tempted, as were so many young seamstresses and other workers, to sell their bodies to make ends meet. Plenty of other groups, both high and low church, ran 'Magdalene' homes for the recovery and retraining of prostitutes. They took the example of Mary Magdalene[7] as an encouragement that repentant prostitutes should be welcomed into the church. For Josephine, this Bible story came to have a double meaning, for she began to see herself in the figure of the woman, identifying at a deep level with 'fallen women'. Like them she had suffered loss; like them she was a sinner; and just as they were invited to, she poured out her resources to honour Christ. Josephine had lost her daughter, and in her grief, she had gained a new drive to reach lost women. She couldn't bring her little Eva back, but she could win the lost to Christ. As she wrote to her sister Hatty, who had by this time had been bereaved of two infant daughters: 'nothing can repair that loss. Still it seems as if God [would] give us souls while he gives us sorrows.'[8]

7. Mary Magdalen was traditionally understood to be the 'woman in that town who lived a sinful life' who anointed Jesus in Luke 7:36-50.

8. From an undated letter, 'To my dear Ann', quoted by Jordan, *Josephine Butler*, 69.

A new home

Two years after Eva's death, the Butlers moved from Cheltenham to Liverpool. It must have been a welcome departure from excruciating physical reminders of the accident and it marked positive progress for George, too. He became headmaster of Liverpool College, a relatively new day school, very large for its time, with around 900 pupils. Whereas Cheltenham was a small, refined spa town, Liverpool was a rapidly developing centre of trade and industry, a place of different cultures and expanding opportunities. The school itself had Jewish and African pupils, alongside English boys and other Europeans. Liverpool's diversity suited Josephine and George well, bringing them new ideas and opportunities for service. Alongside the evident prosperity, as in all growing cities there was great poverty, represented grimly by the huge workhouse on Brownlow Hill, accommodating 5000 destitute or disabled people. Josephine's cousin by marriage, a Baptist minister in Liverpool called Charles Birrell often visited the workhouse to bring pastoral comfort, and it was he who suggested that Josephine should come along and meet the women residing there.

Josephine chose to go to the lowest in the workhouse, those who were picking oakum in dark and damp cellars, some as a punishment for prostitution, drunkenness, theft or violence, others to pay for the shelter they were receiving. What Josephine did once there is remarkable. She sat down and attempted to pick oakum, then, as the women laughed at her, she joined in the mirth, seeing how useless she was with her delicate hands which had never done manual work. They all knew she was different, but somehow she gained their trust and in that very first meeting, she shared Scripture with them, even challenging some to learn some verses by heart. When she returned a week later, one of the women stood and recited John 14:1-27, ending, 'Peace I leave with you; my peace I give you. I do not give to you as the world gives. Do not let your hearts be troubled and do not be afraid.' In awe at this unexpected response, Josephine knelt down, inviting the women to join her and prayed for God's blessing on them all. Her humility is impressive, but perhaps more challenging is her courage. She trusted God enough to take risks, making herself vulnerable, not by speaking about her own difficulties but by listening to others and speaking about Christ. We can do this today. On the streets, in our workplaces and neighbourhoods, in community centres, care homes and our churches, we can stop to listen and speak.

In addition to visiting the oakum sheds, Josephine visited the workhouse infirmary and quickly women in both places became attached to her, seeing a genuineness to her concern and empathy. Within a matter of months, teaching and praying turned into practical care. The Butlers opened their home, just as they had done ten years before in Oxford to 'the most friendless' women and girls when they left the workhouse, often the mentally or physically vulnerable, those who were incurably ill or disabled. When there were too many for their home, George and Josephine rented a house at their own expense to be a 'House of Rest'. Seeing another need a few months later, the Butlers bought a house to be an 'Industrial Home' with the help of wealthy friends. This became a place where poor girls, whose only work was selling sand or waste vegetables on the streets, could work or learn a trade in comfortable circumstances. Josephine's passion to reach prostitutes had not been forgotten though. Some of those who passed through her doors were 'fallen women', and of these one of the first to stay, 'Marion' (a pseudonym), was her favourite. Josephine considered her 'a first fruit' of the work and an example of 'the poor lost dregs of humanity' who would be 'dancing in heaven'.[9]

Marion's story became a model for the great campaign Josephine would undertake, a reminder that there was hope in the work, however hard. A girl from a good farming family, at fifteen Marion had been a servant in a wealthy home. Raped by her employer, she became pregnant and lost her job. Her parents blamed her and turned her away. Marion found work in Liverpool, but her sailor boyfriend deserted her. Broken hearted, Marion recklessly stayed out too late one night and lost her job. Now jobless and homeless, a brothel owner snatched her and put her to work, forcing her to have sex with customers and hiding her from family members who had begun to search for her. Marion became ill with tuberculosis, and she was put out on the streets again and ended up in the workhouse infirmary. There, Josephine spotted her, and seeing that her illness was incurable, took her into her home as a guest. Those women who were taken in by the Butlers were treated as honoured visitors. Josephine nursed them herself, they came downstairs to the drawing room, if they were able, and were treated courteously by George and his sons. There's no surprise that cared for in this way with such acceptance and kindness, Marion and many others who followed responded to the message of Christ's gracious love they heard from Josephine and George's lips. When Marion died a few months later, Josephine made sure she was buried in

9. Josephine Butler, *Josephine Butler*, 64; letter from 1867, quoted by Jordan, *Josephine Butler*, 73.

a white dress, surrounded with camellias, like a bride, a sign to all that she was cleansed of her sins and part of the church, the heavenly bride of Christ.

There were other refuges for prostitutes in Liverpool at this time, but Josephine's was unique in several ways. She welcomed women of any religious background, important in a city with many Irish Catholics. In her homes there was no shade of doing penance for past sins or pressure to respond to the good news of Christ though it was clearly presented; and she seemed to make little distinction between prostitutes and other destitute women, all were invited and cared for. Many died; hardship and disease meant that that on average, once a woman began to prostitute herself, she survived only another five years. George and Josephine had committed to what they saw as the 'revolutionary' character of Christ's teaching early in their marriage and they had found a way to put it into practice in this radical hospitality. Josephine knew that this wasn't enough though. The reasons why women were so vulnerable to exploitation and were treated so harshly if they fell were multiple. Because women had a limited public voice, their concerns could be ignored. With unequal access to education and restricted work opportunities, women were more likely to be impoverished and resort to prostitution to provide for themselves and their families. Knowing this, it was inevitable that she would get involved in early feminist campaigning.

Josephine was an excellent woman to have on your side. She was extremely well connected, both through her large and politically involved family and the wide social circles she and George had moved in. She was also an excellent organiser and powerful writer. Despite her ongoing bouts of severe ill health she became involved with the group pushing for university level education for women and through this access to the professions; with another set of campaigners she had a successful meeting with senior Cambridge academics, asking for access to degree level exams. There was also the campaign for voting rights which she joined and a separate committee working to change the ancient system of coverture, through which a husband legally controlled his wife's income and capital. Using detailed census statistics Josephine argued in her 1868 pamphlet, *The Education and Employment of Women,* that the great numbers of unmarried women (two for every three married women) meant that more opportunities for employment were needed, and pay needed to be raised to lift these many single women out of poverty. This was the time that Ellen Ranyard too, was thinking about expanding opportunities for women as she launched the nursing arm of her mission. A year later, Josephine edited a book of essays by prominent feminists entitled *Women's Work*. Among the ideas in this volume was the suggestion that men should step aside from office work and from skilled jobs like hairdressing: let them do the more physical tasks they were suited to, emigrating if necessary, so that openings could be freed up for frustrated and impoverished women! Josephine's introduction to the volume crystalises her thinking: first, that when women are treated unfairly, men are damaged too, and second, that a woman's natural homeliness, a capacity for bringing order, peace and kindness, can and should be expressed outside the four walls of the home.

Through all her work in these campaigns Josephine revealed her frustration at a society in which many men chivalrously described women as spotless angels but in fact cruelly ruled over them like slave masters. In her writings she proposed another way, based on the dignity and gentleness with which Christ treated women:

> *Search throughout the Gospel history, and observe His conduct in regard to women, and it will be found that the word liberation expresses, above all others, the act which changed the whole life and character and position of the women dealt with, and which ought to have changed the character of men's treatment of women from that time forward.*[10]

Josephine quotes Scriptures to demonstrate this kindness and takes her readers back to Genesis. When God said of Adam 'it is not good for the man to be alone' (Genesis 2:18), she claims a principle of cooperation is established: the world – both then and now – needs men and women, with their different giftings, to work together.

Josephine's Christian convictions about the value of women and her passionate concern for prostitutes came together in the summer of 1869, when she received a request which would redirect her energies. This request came from two doctors and a fellow feminist, but it struck Josephine like a divine calling, plunging her into a few months of prayerful and sorrowful searching. She was being asked to lead a fight against legislation which gave official approval to prostitution in Britain, trapping thousands of women in sexual slavery. This was the opportunity to serve God which she had been waiting for, but which she knew would consume her life.

---

10. Josephine Butler, 'Introduction', in *Women's Work and Women's Culture*, (Macmillan, London: 1869), lix.

12

A Lifetime's Battle

The Contagious Diseases Act had been passed by parliament in 1864 and its scope had been widened twice in 1864 and 1868. The innocuous name of the act and careful timing of debate meant that it had escaped the notice of the general population. Its aim was to protect British soldiers and sailors from disease, so seemed noble and uncontroversial. The details reveal something different. The 'contagious diseases' mentioned are sexually transmitted ones, including gonorrhoea, chlamydia and especially syphilis, which brought long-term symptoms – including lesions, facial disfigurement and excruciating pain – and could lead to an early death and be passed on to children. Syphilis was incurable and it was rife between 1500 and 1900, especially in London, with its more fluid and younger population. Historians estimate that in the 1770s over twenty per cent of the population were infected, by 1907 it was around seven per cent, so in Josephine's time it was probably between these figures. Soldiers and sailors were particularly badly affected, in part because the lower ranks were not allowed to marry and so were likely to be promiscuous.

The result was that sexually transmitted disease injured men almost as much as warfare. It is no wonder that the government wanted to act, but their approach was not to try to prevent men from paying for sex, but to regulate and therefore legitimise prostitution.

A law was established in towns where servicemen were stationed that meant the police could stop any woman they suspected of prostitution and demand that she submit to an internal examination. Evidence of disease led to compulsorily detainment in a 'lock hospital', often part of a workhouse, for 'treatment'.[1] Once the treatment was completed, or if no symptoms were found, the woman would be set free with a certificate declaring her 'clean' and therefore able to offer her body for sale again, but she would be legally required to go back and be examined at regular intervals. A woman who had been discovered on the streets at night, or even in the day, and accused of being a prostitute could resist, claiming she wasn't a prostitute, but this case would have to go before the magistrate. Some women and girls were discharged but others, if they still refused to be examined could be imprisoned for up to six months. Often the women were barely able to read, and had no idea that they had just signed up to regular examination and being listed as a prostitute. There was, of course, no penalty for men who visited these women and who were just as likely to be passing on disease.

---

1. Syphilis couldn't be cured until the formulation of antibiotics in the twentieth century. Internally applying an astringent, antibacterial powder – the treatment of the time – shrank visible signs of the disease, which would return to a latent state of its own accord after a period of months, but continue to do damage to internal organs and cause early death.

Josephine would have known of the Contagious Diseases Act through her work in Liverpool, and would certainly have been opposed to it from its beginning in 1864, but to become a figurehead, confronting this injustice was daunting; she said it was 'so dreadful, so difficult, so disgusting'.[2] It was one thing for a respectable woman to offer mercy and comfort to prostitutes and quite another to speak about sexual issues. In this Victorian period, for women to talk about sex could suggest that they were less than virtuous. In addition, it was rare and often disapproved of for women to address mixed gatherings. Wilberforce had made sure that, though Hannah More and other women were heavily involved in the abolition movement, they did not speak publicly to men. Times were changing, however, and this was a risk Josephine could undertake because of George's support and God's strength.

A plan of attack

The first task was to establish a group and a strategy. Here, Josephine's experience and contacts in other movements stood her in good stead. She formed the Ladies National Association (LNA) to work alongside the men's National Association, and set about gathering signatures for a 'Women's Petition' to be published in the national press on 1 January 1870. The argument was simple and well-argued, based on law, morality and pragmatics. The act was an assault of every Briton's right to 'habeas corpus', the ancient right to freedom; police now had power over women who had committed no crime; it was ineffective – no decline in syphilis was apparent in other places where this kind of legislation had been

2. Josephine Butler, *George Butler*, 219.

enacted; the act punished victims and didn't address the real moral evil of promiscuity. Despite this clarity and the two thousand signatures, the press response was hostile; there was publicity, but not positive progress.

At the same time, Josephine took an unusual step, one which was informed by her own 'rescue work' – she toured northern cities to speak to working men. This audience mostly didn't have the vote and so may have seemed powerless, but they were ready to critique those in power. They were also the husbands, fathers and brothers of women vulnerable to sexual predators and who were being targeted by the act. It was a genius stroke; real feeling was stirred and a number of local campaigning groups were set up. As the new year began, Josephine expanded her tour, speaking to ninety-nine meetings through 1870, some of them men-only, some female-only. More and more local associations were set up and central to many of them was the practice of prayer, in fact, Josephine included written prayers in the campaign literature she produced through her years of the battle. Later that year, after disappointment in Parliament, Josephine travelled to towns affected by the legislation, entering brothels and hospitals to speak to prostitutes. She offered care, gathered evidence and delivered rousing talks.

Josephine threaded Scripture through her speeches and other writings. Unashamedly, she was calling her listeners to a biblical vision of society in which the weak were protected, forgiveness extended to sinners and holiness was demanded of men and women equally. She argued that the laws were based on 'materialist', or atheist, thinking.[3] Josephine saw herself as a

3. Josephine Butler, *Personal Reminiscences of a Great Crusade*, 12.

kind of prophet, titling one pamphlet, *A Voice of One Crying in the Wilderness, 'Prepare the Way for the Lord'*, quoting the description of John the Baptist in Mark 1. Her task, she felt, was through God's power to lead not just individuals but the nation back to the Lord. Conviction of sin was needed, and for this purpose she used stories she had heard first-hand. There was the example of a respectable widow who committed suicide when under suspicion and an innocent girl dragged from her home into a police station. This nineteen-year-old was imprisoned because of her refusal to be examined, then when she relented after five days she was injured in the procedure, only to be told she was, as she had claimed, a virgin. Josephine also used language designed to shock, avoiding the euphemisms of those who defended the act. She implied that examinations were a kind of rape and described the women targeted as 'outcasts', reminding her hearers of God's promises in the Bible to gather up those cast out of society. For her outspokenness she was slandered in the press, but she pressed on. She raised awareness of the horribly low age of consent in Great Britain – just thirteen – which meant that children were being examined and listed as prostitutes. Josephine wasn't the first to attempt to highlight this evil, but by making it part of the campaign against the Contagious Diseases Act, she was significantly strengthening her case, as well as broadening its scope.

In spring 1871, Josephine was able to deliver a petition to parliament with over a hundred times as many signatures as the one she had previously presented. But just like the campaign against the slave trade, convincing parliamentarians that the time was right for change was a difficult matter. A few months later, the Royal Commission's disappointingly mixed report was published; the act should just be moderated not repealed. A loud outcry meant that the Home Secretary had a new proposal: get rid of the unpopular act and replace it with a new law. This law, he felt would make everyone happy: no snatching of women off the streets, but compulsory examination and imprisonment of women convicted of being a prostitute anywhere in the country. It pleased no one, and was dismissed, leaving the National Associations with little to show for all their expense and efforts over three years of campaigning. Josephine was exhausted and close to a break down, but she didn't give up on attempting to influence politicians. She travelled to Pontefract, a Yorkshire mining town, where a military supply base had just been established and the act was being enforced.

Erskine Childers, a naval officer and senior administrator of the act, was standing in Pontefract's by-election. Given her previous support in northern industrial cities, this seemed a good place to try to overturn some of the disappointments experienced in London. Josephine and her male allies turned up in the town to stir up awareness of what Childers had been responsible for, and to encourage voters to switch to his opponent. Aggressive threats meant that she decided to hold a women's meeting in a hayloft on the outskirts of the town. This out of the way place was not hidden enough to deter opponents, however. Just as Josephine began speaking, she noticed smoke curling up through the floorboards. A mob was trying to smoke the women out. It was a terrifying moment: the women were trapped as men climbed up into the loft, shouting and swearing, while others threw stones up at the windows, shattering the glass. Eventually, realising that no one was coming to rescue them, Josephine broke free, jumping through a trapdoor to the floor beneath, followed by her supporters. It was a chilling reminder of the danger of protest, but the drama had an effect. Though Childers did hold onto his seat, it was with a reduced majority and later in 1875, he spoke out in parliament against the Contagious Diseases Act and its subsequent extensions.

Standing with Josephine and the rest of the Association were many Christians, from poor church members to prominent leaders. Although approval was not universal, a great number from different denominations spoke out in support, including two of the most well-known evangelicals of the period, Charles Spurgeon and the Earl of Shaftesbury. Churches lent buildings for meetings and organised prayer. But despite this united force, in 1874, a general election stalled momentum. The Liberals, led by William Gladstone, a Christian who with his wife was involved in the recovery of prostitutes, lost power. Supportive MPs lost their seats and other issues took centre stage in debate. Though for the next five or more years, James Stansfeld, a Liberal MP valiantly represented the cause, there seemed little interest in the House of Commons.

A personal toll

It is easy to forget that through all of the travelling, speech making and writing, while facing such intense hostility, Josephine was a mother of three teenage boys and the wife of a headmaster. She was convinced that leading the campaign was her calling, but God had also given her a family. She needed to be a support to them all and to show herself to be as uncontroversial as possible. So, she played the piano at school concerts, was present at school functions and kept up letter writing, fitting in visits as she could. The pressure to fulfil both sets of responsibilities was overwhelming to a woman who had suffered with health issues since she was a child. In the summer of 1873 Josephine's doctor insisted that she stop everything and rest. She was coughing up blood, was suffering from some kind of gynaecological disorder and had become very thin. It was clear that she was heading for a complete health breakdown. So, as was common at the time, she went south with the family for restorative sunshine. The holiday was funded by donations from her co-campaigners; the Butlers may have come from comfortable, middle-class backgrounds, but they had poured out much of their own income on establishing their women's refuges. They were now the ones in need. Staying in Austria, they were able to take several months to rest, swimming in lakes and walking in the mountains. Josephine particularly enjoyed worshipping in rural churches. Something about the simple devotion she observed reminded her of childhood Methodist services in Northumberland. It was just what she needed for the next challenge awaiting her.

Though she had not long recovered from her serious bout of ill health and a very harsh winter had set in, Josephine crossed the Channel in December 1874 as a representative of the National Association. Though the battle had quietened down in England, Josephine's attention was caught by disturbing noises in Europe. Many European nations had been regulating prostitution far longer and more harshly the British government and now there was talk of a united international approach, promising 'perfect organisation' of the trade in women's bodies.[4] This was terrifying: if nations agreed to

4. Dr Schneider 'Report of Vienna Congress', 49, quoted in Josephine Butler, *Personal Reminiscences of a Great Crusade*, 119.

adopt a shared approach, then it would be so much harder for change to happen anywhere. The Ladies National Association decided they must act to stir supporters in England, as well as try to raise protest in Europe.

George grasped what she was throwing herself into. He and the boys accompanied her for the first half of the trip, and he wrote her a prayer for protection, tucking it into the leaves of her Bible. She must have needed this comfort and encouragement as she made her inquiries in France, Switzerland and Italy; what she discovered was more disturbing than anything she had yet encountered in England. Starting in Paris, Josephine met with people who opposed their country's system, speaking to them in French. She visited a refuge set aside exclusively for children between the ages of four and eleven who had been prostituted. She was allowed into Saint-Lazare, the filthy prison which housed thousands of female criminals alongside prostitutes who were being treated for syphilis. Those who refused examination were confined to straitjackets, and personal washing was forbidden for all the women, ironically on grounds of modesty. What a contrast were the grand offices where she met Monsieur Lecouer, the debonair chief of the Paris 'Morals Police' who had created this system. Later she documented in detail the conversation she had with him. Her fury and frustration rises off the page as she describes how he defended the French policy of licencing brothels and insisted that flirtatious women seduced innocent boys; they were the problem, not men.

Everywhere else Josephine travelled she encountered similar attitudes and heart-rending stories of women exploited and incarcerated. Despite a break mid-way through the trip to see her sister in Naples, her health had been harmed again by long days of intense meetings in which she could only communicate in French, as well as her travels through the Alps in freezing snow. She returned to England ill and emotionally broken. Nightmares and what were probably panic attacks plagued her. She wondered whether anyone would believe the details of what she'd seen in supposedly civilised, Christian Europe. The National Association in England did believe her and provided help. She was given an office and a male secretary to support her in all the work of correspondence, which was greatly increased now she had now international allies. One of these was a gift from God. Before she'd left for the Continent, she had sent a letter to a Monsieur Humbert of Neuchatel in the Swiss Alps, a man suggested to her as a possible supporter. The postman had been confused by the address and delivered the important letter to a different M Humbert. Through God's providence, this Swiss man became Josephine's right-hand man in the European fight. Before the end of 1875, they were able to set up an International Committee to unite forces and share strategies and, in 1877, their first conference was held, supplemented by a whole week of prayer across the continent.

Josephine's efforts bore fruit. She had galvanised opponents to the repressive laws in France, particularly through a book she had written in French. A journalist began to publish stories of the worst excesses of the Morals Police, causing a public outcry. By 1876, Lecouer had been demoted from his powerful position to be a bell ringer in Notre Dame. The system still stood, but this was a small and important sign that change could happen. Josephine understood the slow progress and the horrors through a theological lens, believing this indicated Christ's imminent return, and this gave her hope. In the face of almost indescribable evil, she prayed, as we must, 'Come, Lord Jesus!'[5]

Over the second half of the 1870s, Josephine kept up her writing and speaking. She took every opportunity to warn people against sin, arguing against the sexual double standard, and exhorting listeners to seek Christ. Regular times of rest were necessary though, because of her delicate health; her family must have been glad of these too. George was continuing the demanding work of leading a school and was also involved in the attempt to establish opportunities for higher education in Liverpool. For both of them these holidays spent hiking in the hills and reading together were needed and precious. But even as Josephine attempted to restrict her work, in 1879 – the year Ellen Ranyard died – new evidence of a particularly disturbing form of exploitation was brought to her attention, which would lead to a different season in the campaign.

The war against trafficking

Sex trafficking is a huge problem today; women, girls and boys are lured from their homes in poorer parts of the world to wealthy places with false promises of work. They end up trapped in brothels, often deprived of their passports and effectively enslaved. A hundred and fifty years ago, the same crime was happening in Europe. Josephine's Quaker publisher, Alfred Dyer, discovered that young English girls in Belgium had

5. Unlike Hannah More and Ellen Ranyard, Josephine, along with a growing number in the later nineteenth century evangelical church, held pre-millennial beliefs, convinced that Christ's return would be preceded by disorder and the deterioration of society.

been trafficked for the sex trade and exposed his findings in print in January 1880. The Belgian police and even the British public were sceptical and doubted how something so brutal could possibly be true. More evidence was needed, and so through delicate and traumatic undercover enquiries, involving visits to brothels and prisons in Brussels, Dyer and two others amassed unequivocal proof of an established system of vice. They managed to bring back a number of girls, some of whom were sheltered by Josephine, and she herself signed a deposition of evidence based on what they told her. The very poor or orphans would be promised jobs or even marriage and taken across the channel, where they would be taken for 'examination' and given false documents. Unable to speak the language, having their outdoor clothes taken away, these girls had no means of escape. They were subjected to unimaginable abuse. In the middle of this new campaign, overwhelmed by the horrendous details and unsure what the outcome would be, Josephine remembered that months before:

> *I used to kneel and pray, '... Whatever it may cost us and others, flash light into these abodes of darkness. O send us light, for without it there can be no destruction of the evil.'*

She rebuked herself with the words from the Gospel: 'fools, and slow of heart to believe'.[6] Her prayers were being answered. A court case ensued, and several people were imprisoned. The law was changed in Belgium and thirty-four girls crossed back over

6. Luke 24:25, KJV. Josephine Butler, *Personal Reminiscences of a Great Crusade*, 390.

the Channel to their families. This foreign case stirred further feeling in England and a parliamentary committee again urged a change in the age of consent. God had shone his light on darkness, and the purifying that Josephine prayed so fervently for had come.

For Josephine, progress must have seemed so slow. More than ten years after accepting a leadership role in the campaign and so very many exhausting hours devoted to campaigning, the law had not changed. She found her comfort in God still, seeing in the twists and turns of the campaign, his providences and care. She also continued with her writing, publishing two biographies and a history of the Salvation Army, all of which reflected her heart concern for the poor. By 1883 it looked as if the tide was finally turning. After years of bills being proposed and ignored in parliament, this time there was some optimism. Supporters wrote thousands of letters to their Members of Parliament and on the day of the final vote, gathered across London to pray. Josephine described one event:

> *There were well-dressed ladies, some even of high rank, kneeling together ... with the poorest, and some of the outcast women of the purlieus of Westminster. Many were weeping, but when I first went in they were singing, and I never heard a sweeter sound.*[7]

Josephine rushed between external halls of Parliament where she was able to lobby politicians, the prayer meetings and the Ladies' Gallery, from which she was able to watch the actual

7. Butler, *George Butler*, 175.

voting take place. At last she saw the results announced: they had won! The Contagious Diseases Act had been suspended. But the war wasn't over. Suspension wasn't repeal, and exploitative prostitution was still prevalent. Josephine longed for yet more change and so her last and most daring plan formed.

The exposure of trafficking of young girls to the continent had caused great public outcry, but there seemed little awareness that British girls were vulnerable on home territory. In 1885, a notorious trial was brought to court by the efforts of some of Josephine's allies. A woman who ran three brothels in London was fined only £200, far less than she earned each year from her most famous client, Belgian King Leopold II. She earned so much because many of the 'prostitutes' she sold, were very young indeed. Shockingly, only weeks after the court case, an attempt to raise the age of consent was 'talked out' in the House of Commons, meaning that a vote couldn't be held. This showed that there was complicity in the exploitation of children at the highest level. The campaigners were furious. Josephine's old ally, Dyer, together with key figures in the Salvation Army, planned another investigation. Journalist W.T. Stead, a writer at the Pall Mall Gazette, the equivalent of a modern tabloid, would work with them on a 'secret commission', an undercover operation which would prove that children were being bought and sold in Britain.

By this time, the Butlers had moved to Winchester. They had very little money left, and so a post working in the cathedral had been found for George which meant that they had a lovely home and an income. Within a matter of months of the move, Josephine had established another refuge for women. This time she catered for 'difficult cases': those who were older or incurably ill so couldn't be rehabilitated, as well as some who just didn't fit well into other homes. Rebecca Jarret was one of these. She had been pimped by her own mother at a young age, then become an alcoholic and a brothel owner. She had been converted to Christ through the work of the Salvation Army and was now willing to work with Josephine, whom she loved, and play a part in the 'secret commission'. Rebecca still had contacts and was able to set in motion an approach to a poor, heavy drinking mother; a pound was offered to take her thirteen-year-old daughter away for a job. What this 'work' would involve was clearly implied, though the girl simply thought she was going to become a maid.

Everything worked to plan and, a few days later, young Eliza Armstrong ended up in a room within a brothel in Regent Street, central London. When the journalist Stead entered, Eliza screamed; this was enough, she had not been harmed, but it had been proved that a child could be bought and sold in England. 'Midwives' who examined the girls, the 'fixers', brothel owners and most of all wealthy men, were all guilty. Stead wrote sensational accounts of what had happened in serial form, leading his readers on from one horrific revelation to the next and including other cases and details. As he'd planned, the story shook the capital. This was carefully timed; the reports came out in the week the Commons were to vote on raising the age of consent to sixteen. It worked, and the law was changed, to what we still have today.

However, Josephine and especially Rebecca, who had not long been involved in evangelism among prostitutes, were deeply distressed by their role in such a case. What made everything worse, was that Eliza's parents, shamed by what had happened, made complaints against the Pall Mall Gazette and a court case ensued. Josephine was called as a witness, and Rebecca and Stead, rather than being celebrated for exposing abuse, were tried and found guilty of abducting a child; they spent their Christmas in jail. The next year, 1886, brought better news; at last, after sixteen years of campaigns, the Contagious Diseases Act was repealed.

It still wasn't the end of the battle for Josephine, but it was time to slow down. Her beloved George was in his late sixties and wasn't strong. On their way back from a conference in Scandinavia in 1888, he began with a cold which didn't go away. He was so ill that he made his will, thinking that this was the end. He lived another two years, with ups and downs, but decreasing energy. The International campaign was now fixed on bringing to an end to what were effectively British Army run brothels in India, but Josephine's desire was to nurse her husband and she resisted pressure put on her by her co-workers. The couple travelled south, to try to bring recovery, visiting Josephine's sister in Naples and spending time in the south of France, but by spring 1890 it was clear that George was at the end. As they made their way back to Winchester, George died. Josephine was broken hearted; they had been married for thirty-eight years, and for all that time had been each other's spiritual support. George had been a lover of God's Word; he knew the Psalms by heart and even in his last months had been able to quote Genesis 1 in Hebrew. His faith, perseverance and sacrifice had enabled Josephine to live as she had done. She wondered how she would live without him.

Like other clergy widows, having lost her husband, Josephine now lost her home, tied as it was to his job. She would live for another sixteen years, during which she moved about, unsettled and grieving deeply. A few years in London, then some in Cheltenham interspersed with time on the continent. Her sons were spread about; Charlie returned from South Africa and settled in Cornwall, Georgie and his wife were in Northumberland and Stanley was in Scotland. She spent time with each, enjoying her grandchildren. She sent them letters, pictures and presents, and when with them she loved playing. But portraits show her weakness. She appears shrunken and gaunt despite only being in her sixties or early seventies. Georgie, her eldest son, resented how she had poured out her health and strength on work and not the family. We too might wonder if she got the balance right, but it was a near-impossible juggle.

Despite her ill health and failing sight over the last years of her life, two things remained constant. First was her passion for others to know Christ; she mourned deeply over her sons' disinterest in Christian things and prayed persistently for many others, too, that they might experience the joy of grace. The second was her ongoing concern for the outcasts of society. While in Cheltenham, she expressed her frustration with evangelical culture; Christians went away to gorge on good teaching at conferences, she complained, while all around others starved. Josephine to the last could not ignore the lost and needy and she felt the God's call, not just for herself, but for the whole church to reach out to those who suffered.

Josephine died in 1906 alone with her maid, a few miles away from her birthplace in Northumberland. The Victorian era was over; so much had changed in the seventy-eight years of her life. God had used her loss and suffering to bring the gospel to many women shut out from society, and through her campaigning, cruel laws had been overturned. All of this had come through God's strength. She wrote four days before she died, 'I am holding on in faith. The eternal hand is holding on.'[8]

8. Quoted by Helen Mathers, *The Patron Saint of Prostitutes* (The History Press, Stroud, Gloucester: 2014), 191.

Afterword

And what does the Lord require of you?
To act justly and to love mercy
and to walk humbly with your God. (Micah 6:8)

Rebecca Protten, Hannah More, Ellen Ranyard and Josephine Butler were amazing women and God used them powerfully. But they weren't perfect and their lives were far from easy. Some of their failures and sufferings we know about, others have been lost in the past, forgotten by their friends or glossed over by historians.

Tempting as it is to bypass the difficulties of our heroes, doing so lets us regular believers off the hook. We can excuse ourselves by reasoning, 'I'm not as bright or talented or spiritual as them, so why bother trying to make a difference?' Sometimes, saint-stories make us feel guilty. We beat ourselves up: 'She did all of that, and I can barely get myself through the day; how rubbish am I!' In either case, the focus falls on ourselves and not on the God who calls and equips.

I don't want you to think like that as you finish this book. The four women we've spent time with were part of churches and communities full of Christians like you and me who worked with them in their labours. Those pray-ers, committee members, teachers, nurses, volunteers, petition-signers, ministers, business owners, mothers, brothers and sisters, all contributed to the remarkable progress of God's kingdom in the eighteenth and nineteenth centuries. Just like them, you might not have biographies written about you, but Jesus can use you in the story he is writing today.

Our world is very different. The geographical heart of the church isn't in Europe or America any longer. Technology has transformed all our lives. Cultural values have shifted in very many places. But this is no reason for nostalgia for an easier or somehow more Christian world. We have the same call as Rebecca, Hannah, Ellen and Josephine, and the many who partnered them. In the places we find ourselves, we must speak of Christ and show his mercy. Fierce battles – for the gospel and against evil – might be ours to join. Human trafficking and sex slavery still destroy lives. Inequalities and poverty continue to divide our societies. Many millions haven't heard the gospel. And we mustn't forget that in all the little things of our lives, like our heroes, we are called to suffer and to serve. As we come to Christ, he clothes us in his strength to do his work now.

Acknowledgements

In writing this book I have stood on giants' shoulders.

I am grateful to live in an age when very many primary sources are now available in a digital form. I have also found secondary sources to be a very significant aid. In particular, Jon Sensbach's work on Rebecca Protten and the eighteenth-century Christian culture of the Caribbean has been invaluable. Several biographies of Hannah More exist, among which Anne Stott's and Karen Swallow Prior's have been especially useful. Josephine Butler's story has been told several times. I found Jane Jordan's and Helen Mather's work of great use, and was greatly helped by the excellent unpublished PhD thesis of Amanda Barbara Russell-Jones, which examines Butler's scriptural inspiration. From each of these writers I have learned not only historical details and insights, but also method and passion: thank you all!

While I have been buried in these books, my husband and children have been enormously patient and encouraging, so my thanks goes to them too, of course; you have all helped me more than you know.

Lastly, I must thank my Lord and God. This is his story of grace; he clothed these women with his strength, and the glory must go to him.

10 Publishing
a division of 10 of those.com

10Publishing is the publishing house of **10ofThose**.
It is committed to producing quality Christian
resources that are biblical and accessible.

www.10ofthose.com is our online retail arm selling
thousands of quality books at discounted prices.

For information contact: **info@10ofthose.com**
or check out our website: **www.10ofthose.com**